JB JOSSEY-BASS™
A Wiley Brand

T0327747

90 Great Publicity Ideas for Nonprofits

SECOND EDITION

Scott C. Stevenson, Editor

WILEY

978-1-118-69206-6   ISBN

978-1-118-70434-9   ISBN (online)

90 Great Publicity Ideas
For Nonprofits

— 2nd Edition —

Published by

Stevenson, Inc.

P.O. Box 4528 • Sioux City, Iowa • 51104
Phone 712.239.3010 • Fax 712.239.2166
www.stevensoninc.com

TABLE OF CONTENTS

TABLE OF CONTENTS

90 Great Publicity Ideas for Nonprofits — *2ⁿᵈ Edition*

 ## New- and Old-school Methods Generate Free Publicity

Press releases and public service announcements are always useful free special-event advertising. Internet social networking sites have opened even more avenues. Combine the two to reach the most people.

❑ **Combine diverse talents on a committee**. Find the best writer, artist and Internet whiz to develop a multi-faceted approach to promoting your event. Brainstorming with experienced volunteers is a productive first step.

❑ **Coordinate online resources for maximum effect**. While Facebook and Twitter are available free to anyone with Internet access, promotional advantages can wither on the vine if nobody is monitoring them. Have one knowledgeable person build an event fan page, place sign-up links in e-mail to volunteers and keep track of RSVPs. Ask another to report results to share with the general committee.

❑ **Use a phone tree and short script**. Ask 50 volunteers to call 10 people with a 30-second narrative to fit most voice mail time limits. "Please join us June 25 at 7 p.m. for the first in a series of three summer concerts at Smith Park Pavilion to benefit The Food Pantry. Tickets are $5 for adults and free for children 12 and under." Direct them to your website or office for advance purchase and other information.

❑ **Make mini-fliers to freely distribute**. Create an ad that will fit three to a sheet of letter-sized paper. Ask a printer to donate surplus stock and press time. Contact a direct mail company to see if they will include one in their next mass mailing. Give stacks to volunteers to leave at grocery stores, gas stations and post on community bulletin boards.

❑ **Encourage community participation**. Offer free admission to those donating good used clothing or toys, a case of canned food or any items that help you reach a goal, like stocking a homeless shelter pantry or funding a children's hospital play room. Most media outlets will help spread the word.

 ## YouTube Channel Puts University Research Front and Center

How would you like to share your work and get your message out to 500 people a day? That's what a branded YouTube channel (www.youtube.com) is accomplishing for Purdue University (Lafayette, IN), according to Mike Willis, staff member with Purdue's online experience and emerging technologies group, Office of Marketing and Media.

Purdue's public information and media relations staff started using the channel after noticing other research universities — including the University of California, Berkeley — were doing so successfully.

With the help of the public relations office at Berkeley and YouTube staff, Purdue staff created their own presence on the popular video-sharing site.

In most cases, university officials post videos that are produced in conjunction with news releases put out by the university, Willis says. "Other areas of the university provide some material," he says, "but the basic idea is to not put up video that we would be embarrassed to see on the local TV stations."

They include links to the videos in news releases sent to media and published on Purdue's website. A faculty/staff newsletter also lists links to news releases and videos.

Statistics provided through YouTube analytics (which also tell how viewers locate videos and basic demographic information) show Purdue videos are viewed 500 times per

Setting Up a Branded YouTube Channel

Thinking about how your organization can get started with YouTube (www.youtube.com)?

The site has a program for nonprofits to create their own branded channels.

The program, for eligible nonprofits in the United States and United Kingdom, provides premium branding capabilities and uploading capacity. It also gives the option to drive fundraising, place a call-to-action overlay on videos and post on the YouTube Video Volunteers' Platform to locate a skilled YouTube user to create your video.

For more information or to get started, plus how to maximize your YouTube channel to benefit your cause, visit www.youtube.com/nonprofits.

day. YouTube also uses Purdue's channel as a good example of a university channel.

Willis suggests making sure you have a plan for providing updates and new material for the channel if considering pursuing this form of information sharing.

Source: Mike Willis, Online Experience and Emerging Technologies Group, Office of Marketing and Media, Purdue University, West Lafayette, IN. Phone (765) 494-0371. E-mail: jmwillis@purdue.edu

3 Use Employee Retirement to Highlight Your Organization

When a longtime employee or volunteer retires, go beyond the cake and gold watch to share the milestone with the community. Here are some ideas:

✓ **Send an interview/press release to media**. Include the person's career path, how he/she participated in milestones like construction of facility landmarks or pitched in during a blizzard when 200 people were stranded in your gym. A few key memories can lead reporters to other interesting questions for their own interviews.

✓ **Host a community reception with dignitaries**. Include former board members, past presidents, and local officials who may know the honoree. Take plenty of photographs of the retiring employee with VIPs to send to appropriate publications (hometown newspapers, college alumni magazines, trade journals).

✓ **Recognize achievement**. Honor the person's profession-al achievements with a separate award, such as Spirit of Excellence that has nothing to do with the approaching retirement. When you announce their departure as news, they may benefit from the increased attention that comes from name recognition — and you do want to honor them professionally while the opportunity exists.

✓ **Celebrate seniors online**. The power of social media was recently shown when one dedicated fan of 88-year-old actress Betty White launched a Facebook fan page to encourage NBC to ask White to host "Saturday Night Live." You can do the same to honor employees who have been with your company for 50 years.

✓ **Host a party to launch their next career**. Your retiring comptroller plans to open a crafts boutique or buy a coffee shop after dedicating 40 years to your organization. Approach this retirement as a kick-off party for his or her next venture for a new media-generating twist.

4 President's Journal Connects With Members, Community

If building connections within and beyond your membership is a priority, consider a regular newsletter column, monthly e-mail, web log or other ongoing correspondence written by one or more of your organization's key players.

For four years, Charlotte Keim, president of the Marietta Area Chamber of Commerce (Marietta, OH), has posted her thoughts, insights, dreams for the chamber, plus shared information and feedback from members and movers and shakers through her President's Journal, a professional blog hosted on the chamber's website (http://mariettachamber.com/3?newstype=2).

The president's journal features 500- to 600-word essays on topics both occupational and personal. Because the journal is open to the public, its tone differs significantly from other chamber communications, the author notes.

"There is less hard information and more thoughts for reflection and perspective," Keim says. "I try to balance heavy and light, business and non-business, local and regional. To build those personal connections, it helps to have something for everyone."

Recent articles amply demonstrate this variety of subject matter, ranging from the personal "Thankful for Living in Marietta — My Hometown" to the topical "Marietta Chamber Supports Issue 2 & Marietta School Bond" and the historical "Growing Our Economy — A Tale of Marietta From 1921."

For leaders interested in trying such an approach, Keim offers the following tips.

❏ **Don't start if you don't like writing (at least a little)**. "If it's a chore for you to write something, it will be a chore for others to read it," she says.

❏ **Don't commit to a strict schedule**. Though Keim aims for biweekly postings, she recommends a looser approach for those just beginning.

❏ **Write several entries before posting the first**. "Having a bank of five or six articles will give you some breathing room when things get busy."

Check out the President's Journal — the online blog written by Charlotte Keim, president of the Marietta Area Chamber of Commerce (Marietta, OH) — at http://mariettachamber.com/3?newstype=2

❏ **Take notes**. "Most people underestimate how difficult it is to think of ideas when staring at a blank piece of paper," Keim says. "Jotting down interesting stories, statistics and bits of news provides a good source of inspiration."

And a final piece of advice? Keep things positive, advises the chamber president. "Everyone has challenges, and that should be acknowledged," Keim says. "But people are looking for hope and optimism, too. That's what they really respond to."

Source: Charlotte Keim, Marietta Area Chamber of Commerce, Marietta, OH. Phone (740) 373-5176.
E-mail: keim@mariettachamber.com.
Website: www.mariettachamber.com

5   Popular Video Game Adds Pop to Media Spot, Value for Sponsor

Staff at The Louisville Zoo (Louisville, KY) used a video game's popularity to generate media attention for the zoo's annual World's Largest Halloween Party.

Kara Bussabarger, public relations manager, works with local stations to organize early-morning live remotes at the zoo to promote the event. In 2008, event sponsor Best Buy helped add to the fun of such a live remote, as staff set up a Guitar Hero video game system. The TV reporter played the game live on the air, interacted with Best Buy employees and talked about their involvement in the upcoming party.

Bussabarger says that some events definitely lend themselves to creativity for publicity and media, which makes for a win-win situation for the zoo and the sponsor.

Source: Kara Bussabarger, Public Relations Manager, The Louisville Zoo, Louisville, KY. Phone (502) 238-5331. E-mail: kara.bussabarger@louisvilleky.gov

6   Use Well-known Faces to Garner Publicity

Do you have graduates, donors, staff, active volunteers or supporters who are particularly well-known?

Spotlight them in your promotional materials to generate publicity for your organization.

"We feature successful graduates of Trinity in our admissions recruiting materials, including Cathie Black, president of Hearst Magazines, which publishes Oprah magazine, Good Housekeeping and many other familiar names among magazines," says Ann Pauley, vice president for institutional advancement, Trinity Washington University (Washington, D.C.). "We want to show prospective students the kinds of successful role models that Trinity Washington University educates."

Showcasing successful alumni and others connected to your organization can have longlasting positive effects.

"In fall 2007, we enrolled the largest freshman class in 40 years," and in fall 2008, had an all-time enrollment high, Pauley says. "Obviously, there are many factors involved, including hard work on the part of our admissions staff, strategic communications, careful follow up, successful open houses, etc. But marketing materials are definitely a factor, and featuring successful graduates in those materials is part of that strategy."

The university has been featuring outstanding alumni in marketing materials for many years in a variety of ways, including:

- Admissions materials, including brochures and newsletters, include photos, interviews and descriptions of these stellar graduates' achievements.

- On the university's homepage, a rotating Profiles of Success feature, which includes stories and photos of successful, well-known graduates.

When spotlighting a well-known member of the community in publicity efforts, be sure to obtain permission to use the person's likeness, quotes and other personal information. You may wish to meet with them in person for interviews or photo sessions.

Pauley says the university occasionally arranges for photo sessions with featured graduates to obtain images for certain materials, in addition to using photos of the graduates already used in feature articles in the university magazine.

She advises choosing people who are at different levels of their career and who will appeal to a wide audience.

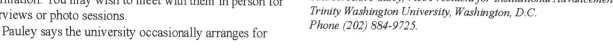

Content not available in this edition

Along with using the highly visible Cathie Black, they have also featured Perita Carpenter, a producer for ABC News who is a more recent graduate.

"High school students will relate better to more recent graduates, but they are also impressed by those graduates who are at the top of their careers," says Pauley.

Tying successful individuals to your organization will show the community how hardworking and unique you are.

"We receive positive feedback from prospective students, parents and guidance counselors when they see who some of our successful graduates are," says Pauley. "That gives them confidence that Trinity provides a high quality educational experience with an emphasis on women's leadership skills."

Source: Ann Pauley, Vice President for Institutional Advancement, Trinity Washington University, Washington, D.C. Phone (202) 884-9725.

7   Personalize Screen Savers

Personalized screen savers are a cost effective, eye-catching way to publicize your organization.

"We began offering downloadable Calvin screen savers in March 2001," says Phil de Haan, director of communications and marketing, Calvin College (Grand Rapids, MI). "The idea was simply to add something fun and entertaining to our website while connecting people with the college."

They used Adobe Flash and FlashForge by Goldshell Digital Media to create the screen savers at minimal cost, says de Haan. While a license for FlashForge was approximately $60 in 2001, he says it is now freeware.

Luke Robinson, Web manager, came up with the idea for the screen savers, which he describes as "the next logical step after creating downloadable wallpaper for PC desktops."

He worked with the graphic designer and a student to develop the screen savers. They were created relatively quickly, with the first one taking the most time.

"It took about eight hours of development to find the right screen saver authoring application and to develop the website," says Robinson. "The student who created the Flash animation spent about eight hours learning how to create a seamless loop and transitions. Afterward, each new screen saver was a matter of replacing artwork, exporting a new Flash movie and authoring the screen saver in Goldshell."

They used images from several sources, including the campus wall calendar and online photo galleries of campus events and academic pursuits.

To publicize screen savers, officials sent an e-mail to faculty and students via the campus listserv and added a link to the homepage of the college website. The screen savers are also used in the computer labs and campus information stations.

Robinson says the most challenging aspect of the project is finding exceptional images. Once such images are identified, he says, let them take center stage, keeping logos and other information minimal.

Sources: Phil de Haan, Director of Communications and Marketing; Luke Robinson, Web Manager; Calvin College, Grand Rapids, MI . Phone (616) 526-6475 (de Haan) or (616) 526-8686 (Robinson). E-mail: dehp@calvin.edu (de Haan) or lrobinso@calvin.edu (Robinson)

8   Think Creatively to Maximize News of Major Achievements

When your nonprofit is recognized for its high level of service or contributions to the community, don't let the publicity end with a news release announcing the honor. Do all you can to spread the news throughout your service region and to your supporters.

While not every award will result in broad media coverage, you can do several things to increase public awareness of your recent achievements. For example:

❑ **Create award icons for Web and e-mail.** Develop a design template for a digital logo like Top 10 Best Hospitals for 2009 or Best Environment for Children with the name of the awarding organization. Use them on your website and in all e-mail communications for a designated period of time, updating as needed.

❑ **Buy advertising or use public service announcements (PSAs).** TV, newspaper or radio advertising is an effective way to thank the organization or people responsible for your success while simultaneously announcing your achievement.

❑ **Target specific reporters.** When a professional group singles out a specific department or service area in your organization for excellence, look to share this good news with the appropriate media outlets. For instance, an Excellence in HR Services honor may make an excellent article for your local business journal or industry trade paper.

❑ **Highlight individuals.** If specific individuals or groups of volunteers were the impetus behind your organization's honor, contact their respective churches, schools or alumni group with the good news. Smaller publications that run once a month or less are often more fully read than daily papers because recipients are targeted.

❑ **Use electronic e-mail services and newsletters.** Services like Constant Contact® (www.constantcontact.com) and Network for Good (www.networkforgood.org) enable you to send attractively presented announcements to large audiences. Include media contacts in your lists, and use attention-getting subject lines like "Selected Among Best Managed Facilities by National Magazine."

❑ **Consider unique advertising methods.** Bus benches, vehicle wraps and billboards can be cost-effective ways to attract positive attention, particularly when your contract permits changing the design or copy as you receive other awards. The brevity of the message "Ranked #1" lends itself to a medium people will see while driving or waiting in traffic.

Collaboration Helps Address Serious National Health Issue

Take on a headline-grabbing issue and you'll be sure to garner positive press while furthering your mission for the good of others and your community.

To address the problem of childhood obesity, which has reached epidemic proportions in the United States, officials with the Nationwide Children's Hospital (Columbus, OH) established the Nationwide Children's Hospital Fitness And Nutrition (F.A.N.) Club in 2008. The club is part of the hospital's pediatric obesity initiative to help third, fourth and fifth graders experience fun activities to keep them fit and healthy through physical activity and education. The after-school and summer club includes activities such as strength training, games, flag football, stretching, cardio-aerobic activities and nutrition, and there is no cost to club participants, says Doug Wolf, an athletic trainer with the hospital's Children's Sports Medicine Team.

While two area schools got on board at the program's start, plans are to expand the program. In the current school year, the F.A.N Club is setting up shop in a third school, thanks to a partnership with Mt. Carmel College of Nursing (Columbus, OH) and grant funding.

"We aren't just focused on children who are our patients, but also on opportunities to partner within our community to impact children's long-term health," Wolf says. "Combating and preventing pediatric obesity is a great example of an issue where we have expertise, strong community partners and resources in place to focus on wellness promotion now to help prevent chronic conditions for our F.A.N. Club children later in life."

The program is paying off, with young participants able to do 30 percent more sit-ups and enjoying a 100 percent increase in aerobic capacity.

Wolf's biggest piece of advice for nonprofits looking to launch a community service project similar to the F.A.N. Club? Have a strong core group overseeing the project that includes people from a wide range of backgrounds who are committed to forming collaborations and partnerships to drive the success and sustainability of the program.

Source: Doug Wolf, Athletic Trainer Children's Sports Medicine, Nationwide Children's Hospital, Columbus, OH.
E-mail: Douglas.Wolf@NationwideChildrens.org.
Phone: (614) 355-6007.

 Get Valuable TV Exposure for Your Cause

Every nonprofit organization has newsworthy events, but few promote them through TV exposure. This can be an exciting prospect. Don't be intimidated by TV. Your story idea does not have to be as earth shattering as the latest quake.

It helps if you have a unique angle, an interesting character or an out-of-the-ordinary theme. Most TV stations set aside daily free public service broadcast time. Some have special segments dedicated to interviewing an event organizer. Here's how to get on the air:

✓ **Contact television stations.** From the community affairs director, request guidelines for submitting a story idea or publishing an event. Is it communicated by letter, e-mail, fax or phone? Obtain the name of the person to whom you should submit your proposal, along with the correct phone number or e-mail address.

✓ **Meet submission deadlines.** Most TV stations need six to eight weeks' notice. If your big event occurs in April, you need to inform the TV station by February. If it's a human interest story in progress, contact them immediately.

✓ **Get programming guidelines.** What type of project does the TV station accept? For example, some channels offer free exposure to nonprofit entities. Others broadcast only community-related events or qualifying activities such as performances or fundraising events. Still others look for emotionally charged human interest stories.

✓ **Use the community calendar.** These calendars appear as text on the screen, accompanied by an announcer's voice. It is relatively easy to get your event or recruiting activity included here. Put all the details in writing, include a publish-by date, and your name as a contact.

✓ **Watch the station.** Analyze public service segments to learn what catches a programming manager's attention. Note time of day programs air and what they feature.

✓ **Be innovative.** Every organization has newsworthy clients or employees or an inspiring goal. For example: "80-year-old twins volunteer at Literacy Center" or "Donated hours exceed 20,000 for the first time in Nature Center's history" or "He once drove an army tank. Now he drives a Meals-on-Wheels van."

✓ **Be persistent.** As one station manager put it, "Submit everything you think our audience would be interested in. The squeaky wheel will eventually get greased. If we see your proposals enough times, we'll probably get around to doing a story on you."

✓ **Show appreciation.** If you do land a TV spot, request a copy. Be sure you follow up with a thank-you note — not an e-mail but a handwritten note. So few people do this that you will be remembered fondly the next time you have a hot piece of news.

11 Hire the Right Firm to Distribute Your Press Releases

Are you looking for a firm to distribute your press releases and media advisories for you? Take advantage of the free trials offered by many of the companies.

Free trials will give you the best information you need to make your choice, says Tom Evelyn, director of media relations, Bucknell University (Lewisburg, PA), who has taken advantage of free trials on behalf of his organization.

A free trial with a press release distribution company will provide you with:

✓ **The opportunity to compare side-by-side.** Always ask for free trials from more than one company. This ensures that you really have something to compare. Other companies may do the job better. If you only evaluate one, you'll never know.

✓ **The chance to test drive customer service.** Evelyn says he asks for trial runs of at least two weeks so he can find problems and ask the companies to solve them. "The response to these requests can tell you a lot about the level of customer service you might receive if you sign on."

Press Release Distribution Companies

Want to give a press release distribution firm a try? Check out these to get you started:

❏ PRWeb — www.prweb.com
❏ Business Wire — www.businesswire.com
❏ Market Wire — www.marketwire.com
❏ 24-7 pressrelease.com — www.24-7pressrelease.com
❏ PR.com — www.pr.com

✓ **A way to determine if they provide the information you need and whether the service is user-friendly.** Evelyn says it is also important to get recommendations from your colleagues about the services they use and if they would renew their contracts with those companies. You can also check out media relations listservs. Evelyn says such conversations are a frequent topic on many of them.

Source: Tom Evelyn, Director of Media Relations, Bucknell University, Lewisburg, PA. Phone (570) 577-3698. E-mail: tevelyn@bucknell.edu

12 50th Anniversary Celebrates Members, Community

Focus your milestone celebrations on the people who made them possible.

Staff at the Phoenix Art Museum (Phoenix, AZ) created a comprehensive plan to celebrate the organization's 50th anniversary with its membership and community.

Festivities begin with the pARTy 2009. The annual black-tie gala drew more than 750 museum friends and supporters for cocktails in the Jacquie and Bennett Dorrance Sculpture Garden, a gourmet dinner in the Ellen and Howard C. Katz Wing for Modern Art and dancing to live music by The Peter Duchin Orchestra in the Cummings Great Hall.

To further celebrate the 50th anniversary, museum staff:

❏ **Created a written history of the organization:** The "Fabulous at 50" book showcased the esteemed history of the organization and was unveiled at the pARTy. The compilation was created within six months and contains photos and a historical account of the growth of the museum.

❏ **Honored members with a special event:** The 50th Anniversary Member Celebration, Party Like It's 1959 event was held Nov. 21, 2009, the actual 50th anniversary of the museum, and featured as special guests, 30 couples who were members of the museum for 50 years or more. Specialty items and offerings from the 1950s era put guests in the time and place when the museum first came to be. A movie screening featuring

"Some Like It Hot" for adults and "Sleeping Beauty" for the younger crowd — both box office hits in 1959, the year the museum opened — offered a nostalgic retrospective. A barbershop quartet and brass ensemble offered musical entertainment reminiscent of the 1950s. Special architecture tours provided a detailed physical accounting of the museum's growth over five decades. Candy, games and toys for children at the event, such as hula hoops, were all geared to the 1950s theme.

❏ **Hosted an event honoring major donors and members:** Major donors and Circles of Support members attended a special exhibition opening reception for the museum's 50/50: Fifty Gifts Celebrating Fifty Years exhibition, which unveiled more than 300 new pieces acquired by the museum in honor of its 50th anniversary.

❏ **Offered a public celebration to the greater Phoenix community:** Beyond membership events to mark this major milestone, staff also created a public celebration to coincide with the Downtown Phoenix First Friday event that features special exhibits by area art galleries and museums. The free Friday night fiesta offered the museum a way to share its anniversary with the public.

Source: Tammy Stewart, Membership and Visitor Services Manager, Phoenix Art Museum, Phoenix, AZ. Phone (602) 257-2124. E-mail: Tammy.Stewart@phxart.org. Website: www.phxart.org

13   Submit-a-story Idea Gives Audience a Say in Coverage

Tap a vested source of story ideas by turning to your constituents — clients, volunteers, members, donors and staff, to name a few — for their perspective on what makes your organization great.

After Bucknell University (Lewisburg, PA) staff redesigned their website in 2008, they quickly found one of the more successful additions to be its Submit a Story Idea link, says Tom Evelyn, director of media relations.

"Our audiences were sometimes confused about how we generated story ideas and how they could share their ideas," Evelyn says. "We thought that providing a simple online form would help guide those readers who wanted to share story ideas but weren't sure where to start."

The link, which averages a couple of submissions each week, provides constituents a direct connection to the communications staff so they can have a say in the news the university covers.

Though the number of ideas isn't overwhelming, Evelyn says promptness is important. "Some stories have a limited shelf life, so you have to be prepared to check the submissions regularly. They require regular attention to ensure timely responses."

He also says that the benefits far outweigh the risks. "It's impossible to cover all of the great stories out there, but the Submit a Story Idea function helps by providing our audiences with a mechanism to tell us about stories we might not hear about otherwise. And in the process, our audiences feel more involved in helping the university tell the world about Bucknell and its excellence."

There is the potential to offend someone by not picking up their story idea, but Evelyn says that is manageable as long as you are proactive. To that end, Bucknell's form includes the following wording: "If a suggested story opportunity fits with our planning, a member of the communications staff will contact the individual." The staff also tries to offer alternative local outlets for stories that may not merit widespread publication.

Check out the link on the Web page for Bucknell's Division of Communications (http://www.bucknell.edu/x4728.xml) and click on the Submit A Story link.

Source: Tom Evelyn, Director of Media Relations, Bucknell University, Lewisburg, PA. Phone (570) 577-3698. E-mail: tevelyn@bucknell.edu.

14   Make a Radio Pitch That Works

The better prepared you are to add value to your pitch for free radio air time, the more likely your pitch will be a success.

Pennie Gonzalez, special events director, Albany Broadcasting (Latham, NY), says charities should understand that radio stations get hundreds of requests each year for in-kind advertising and donations.

"When we say 'no,' it's nothing personal, but we really need to pick and choose." Gonzales says. With that in mind, she says organizations must have something of value to offer the radio station in exchange for a promotion.

Opportunities that offer the most value to radio stations, she says, are:

❑ On-site displays and banners at events.

❑ Radio station logo on collateral and marketing materials.

❑ Access to events that may provide good networking opportunities.

Inviting one of the station's personalities to serve as master/mistress of ceremonies, host or introduce an event also adds value for the radio station by giving its celebrities exposure to potential new audiences, Gonzalez says.

Jeanne Charters, Charters Marketing (Asheville, NC), agrees that nonprofits need to offer that something extra to make those media pitches successful.

"It's a tough time right now," Charters says. "Nonprofits have to set themselves apart from all of the other people clamoring for money the same way Lowe's has to set itself apart from The Home Depot."

Be sure to do your homework before making your pitch to prospective radio stations, Charters advises, "Target the proper demographic, establish your compelling selling niche and hammer that point in everything you do."

Further, she says, compare markets and mediums by knowing how to talk cost per rating point (CPP). CPP is the cost to reach 1 percent of a specified target audience with an ad through a specific media vehicle. Having that knowledge can help you evaluate how efficiently one medium is in comparison to others.

Sources: Jeanne Charters, Charters Marketing, Asheville, NC. Phone (828) 274-3003. E-mail: jcharters@bellsouth.net
Pennie Gonzalez, Special Events Director, Albany Broadcasting, Latham, NY. Phone (518) 786-6757.
E-mail: pgonzalez@albanybroadcasting.com

15 Reach Out to Media for Dream Coverage

Waiting for that dream story (you know… the one that both accurately and emotionally captures the good work your nonprofit organization does) to appear magically in the media? Well, why not take the bull by the horns and take your story to the media?

Invite a few hand-selected reporters to your facility and offer them an exclusive behind-the-scenes look at your organization. Bringing reporters on site allows you to control the discussion.

Bring them in individually, rather than as a group, and give them a tour of your facility. More importantly, give them access to key programs, departments or individuals (e.g., the CEO or executive director, key researchers, top board members, etc.). Allow time for one-on-one interviews. Also, be sure to emphasize the aspects you want covered in the story.

You'll find that this approach will help yield long-term results with media coverage.

16 Reinforce Your Brand With Striking Images

Display striking photos that show your organization's mission in action to further your branding efforts and inspire staff, visitors, donors and volunteers.

In December 2008, staff with Lutheran World Relief (LWR) of Baltimore, MD hung three high-impact photos in their lobby. The 20 X 30-inch, color framed images (shown at right) show participants in LWR development projects around the world.

"The primary reason we put up the photos was to reinforce our brand identity as a global organization," says Emily Sollie, director, communication & media relations. "We also hoped they'd be inspirational in a broad sense, capturing happy, self-empowered people from different cultures and contexts, and in various stages of life, who all have a brighter outlook on the future. The hope is that the photos help remind people, both staff and visitors, of our organizational mission and vision, and ultimately why we do the work that we do."

Communications staff selected about 40 photos from their image database as candidates for the display. Eight staff members reviewed the photos and made recommendations as to which should be displayed.

"The leadership team endorsed those recommendations and the photos were approved for display by the building committee," says Daniel Lee, director, marketing. The images were enlarged by a print shop and matted and framed by a local framing business.

"The anecdotal feedback received thus far has been overwhelmingly positive," he notes. "Our staff and guests appreciate the change in decor, but especially like how captivating and inviting the new images are."

When selecting images to display in your lobby or other area, the LWR officials say, look for high quality images capable of being enlarged without loss of quality. Be sure you have permission of the subjects to use their images in a promotional manner.

Finally, consider asking staff members, participants, volunteers and others to weigh in on which images they feel represent your brand in a positive and inspiring way.

Source: Daniel Lee, Director, Marketing; Emily Sollie, Director, Communication & Media Relations; Lutheran World Relief, Baltimore, MD. Phone (410) 230-2800. E-mail: DLee@lwr.org or ESollie@lwr.org

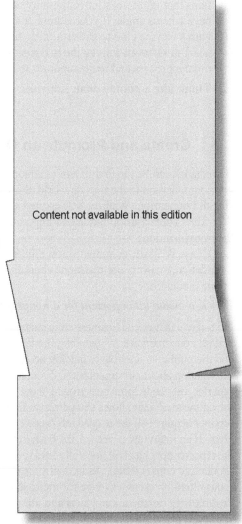

Content not available in this edition

Images of persons whose lives are made better thanks to the work of Lutheran World Relief take center stage at the organization's Baltimore, MD headquarters.

Ideas to Score Free Publicity

One of the best ways to attract free positive media coverage is with a news angle about your cause that also satisfies a public need for information or fills an assignment editor's need for a timely good news story.

To develop a strategic plan to attract coverage that can spread the good word about your cause:

❏ **Keep a file of news topics that are timeless — known as evergreens — at ready access.** Examples include a list of resident experts in areas such as psychological health, nutrition, children's safety or finances. Turn your expert's advice into a short article with information the whole community may value. Send copies to media contacts to use as they see fit.

❏ **Share your volunteers or staff.** Charitable organizations that join forces for community betterment often have a news angle. If your alumni or auxiliary teams with a service club to gather holiday toys for children in need, think of an activity the two groups will hold during the process and invite reporters to see them in action.

❏ **Think like a photo editor.** Activities involving smiling children interacting with seniors or people doing something outside of their comfort zone for a good cause (think bank-president-turned-Santa or mayor volunteering for a hands-on cleanup effort) are sure to capture the media's eye.

❏ **Co-sponsor a community-wide effort.** Offering your organization's strengths in support of an overall effort shows cooperation and that you recognize the good that can be accomplished as part of a team. Newspapers, TV or radio stations often are part of such teams and list other participating organizations as they use their medium to highlight their own involvement.

❏ **Appeal to a reporter's sense of adventure.** Think of situations involving your organization that might make a good story for a reporter, such as inviting them to spend an afternoon in a research laboratory observing scientists, at a trauma center watching healthcare professionals in action or in a homeless shelter kitchen as staff prepare a meal. The perspective they gain will make a good story for them, and bring your services to the public eye.

 Create and Promote an Online Media Kit

A media kit can be the first line of communication about your organization to the outside world. Staff with the Kansas Health Foundation (Wichita, KS) created an online media kit that offers contact information and important details about their organization.

Chase Willhite, communication officer at Kansas Health Foundation, answers our questions about the organization's online media kit:

Why is a media kit important for a nonprofit organization?

"In today's fast-paced business environment, it is important that all constituencies — including media, partners, grantees and the public — are able to quickly access valuable information about our organization. From a media lens, if a reporter just needs some background about our organization, the online media kit allows that person to find basic facts.... If a reporter acquires all the needed information from the media kit, great. If an interview is needed, the background information the reporter now has will hopefully lead to a richer, more productive conversation. Additionally, organizations should focus attention on any avenue for increased transparency dealing with organizational facts and information."

What are the most important components of the media kit?

"As with most of our publications, resources, or communication strategies, the media kit is designed to answer the questions, 'Who are we?' and 'What do we do?' Our website, in its entirety, provides a wealth of information on our grant making, our history and other points of interest. The media kit, though, provides a quick reference for answering those questions, and potentially leading the reader to explore more about our organization throughout the website. As far as specific components, we include management team information with links to staff biography pages, contact information, mission, a brief history and an overview of our focus areas as well as funding priorities."

What specific tips do you have for completing a streamlined media kit?

1. "Ask yourself, 'What are the most important elements of our organization we'd like the public to know?'

2. "Make sure the entire online page can be read and digested quickly, while still providing the needed information.

3. "Use a short paragraph or bullet-point format to make the information easier to read.

4. "Offer concise details."

Source: Chase Willhite, Communication Officer, Kansas Health Foundation, Wichita, KS. Phone (316) 262-7676. E-mail: cwillhite@khf.org. Website: www.kansashealth.org

19   Securing Media Coverage In Changing Media Market

With certain media markets dwindling, including doors closing on some newspapers, how do you make sure your story gets out?

"It's more important than ever to find a real point of differentiation in the news you're offering," says Nicole Pitaniello, assistant vice president for public relations, Albany Medical Center (Albany, NY).

Pitaniello says she used this strategy when pitching a story similar to one a local paper had already picked up on in brief. The pitch was about new technology that would enable people with certain neurological conditions to communicate better. The reporter was hesitant to follow through with a feature piece because of the prior story. Pitaniello says she convinced the reporter it would be worthwhile because of the value to the paper's readers.

"I argued that if one of my family members had one of these conditions and there was something out there that could help improve their quality of life, I'd want to know about it. And a story like the one I was pitching could make it real for people," Pitaniello says. "It's really all about selling them on why it's important for their readers to know this information, not why it's important ... to get your story told."

Source: Nicole Pitaniello, Assistant Vice President for Public Relations, Albany Medical Center, Albany, NY. Phone (518) 262-3421. E-mail: PitaniN@mail.amc.edu

20   Teaming Up Expands Reach of Awareness Campaign

A well-planned, well-executed awareness-building campaign can significantly boost your support base along with your community profile.

Such a campaign by Gilda's Club Capital Region New York (Latham, NY) helped boost membership by 127 percent.

Edwin Graham — president/CEO of the organization that creates welcoming communities of free support for persons with cancer, their families and friends — says he and his staff formulated a plan to raise awareness because they believed people just didn't understand the mission of Gilda's Club (named for actress/comedian Gilda Radner, who died of cancer).

The result was a concentrated effort that allowed them to double their member numbers in a short time while also boosting awareness of their organization's services.

Graham explains what made the awareness campaign successful:

❑ **Getting creative.** Some $80,000 in donated services allowed them to create an award-winning DVD to give to cancer patients through oncologists' offices. Graham says, "We didn't want it too spit-polished though, so we went directly to members for a conversation from the heart and tried to represent all of the different faces of Gilda's Club."

❑ **Collaborating.** Gilda's Club partnered with the American Cancer Society (ACS) as a natural progression of their existing collaboration through a local consortium. "Gilda's is a complement to what ACS does, so it didn't make sense for both of us to be in the same doctors' offices, possibly confusing patients," he says. Now ACS staff give Gilda's Club DVDs to newly diagnosed patients.

❑ **Knowing the source.** Graham says the most important

Doctor's Prescription Boosts Awareness

Edwin Graham, president and CEO, Gilda's Club Capital Region New York (Latham, NY), shares another idea for boosting awareness, especially for organizations that provide services to people who are sick:

Give healthcare providers note pads that resemble prescription pads, but are printed with an organization-specific message rather than a prescription. The idea is for them to share information about your organization with appropriate patients.

The outreach plan for Gilda's Club (detailed at left) included giving prescription pads preprinted with "Go to Gilda's Club," to doctors who, in turn, gave patients the preprinted prescription to visit the cancer support organization when appropriate.

Graham says the doctor's nod of support was just what some people needed to visit the organization and take advantage of its support services.

factor in any outreach campaign is to know who your referral sources are and build relationships with them. "If you have no money and no means, it's still OK. You really need to connect with the folks who see value in what you do and are in contact with the people who need it."

❑ **Committing to keeping your members.** Once you develop relationships, commit to keeping them going, says Graham: "Turnover can be high. You can't meet with folks just once and expect them to remember what you have to offer."

Source: Edwin Graham, President/CEO, Gilda's Club Capital Region New York, Latham, NY. Phone (518) 782-9833. E-mail: egraham@gccrny.org

21 Promote Your Stories on Others' Websites

Seek out ways to get your news stories on websites other than your own.

"I promote use of our stories and press releases on the websites of affiliated organizations," says Aubrey Streit, director of communications, Bethany College (Lindsborg, KS). "For example, we recently wrote and distributed a press release about a service learning trip our students took to help with recovery efforts in Greensburg, KS. We received coverage on several key sites, including the National Association of Intercollegiate Athletics and Central States Synod of the Evangelical Lutheran Church in America (ELCA)."

Streit targets organizations that have a link to the school. "The Central States Synod of the ELCA is one of the synods that supports our school, so the readers of their site may already have an interest in Bethany College," she says.

She also recommends listening to people in and around your organization regarding websites they frequently read.

To streamline the process of reaching out to websites beyond those of media contacts, Streit and her staff added e-mail addresses for other appropriate websites to their media distribution list to make it easy to e-mail them relevant news releases.

"What we gain from story placements on the Web are wider exposure on the Internet, as well as exposure to targeted audiences of readers. These readers get referred back to our Web page," says Streit.

"Because Web links are easy to communicate, we routinely share press coverage in our on-campus e-mail newsletter," she says. "This helps people on campus realize that the stories they contribute to do matter and get read, and helps them take pride in Bethany."

In addition, she says, sending stories to nonprofits affiliated with the college's mission has strengthened relationships with those important organizations.

Pitching your stories to other organizations is no different than pitching to media contacts, Streit says, "Know the website, have an idea of who its readers are, and be able to connect your story to the site's purpose and readers."

Source: Aubrey Streit, Director of Communications, Bethany College, Lindsborg, KS. Phone (785) 227-3380, ext. 8274.
E-mail: streita@bethanylb.edu

22 Blogs Bring Student Voices to the Recruitment Process

Imagine being able to follow the lives of several students for a whole year, for an up-close and personal look at what a college is really like, before deciding whether you want to go there.

That's what staff at Bucknell University (Lewisburg, PA) created with "A Year in the Life" blogs (http://yearinthelife.blogs.bucknell.edu).

Molly O'Brien-Foelsch, senior writer, says the concept started in 2004. Initial versions chronicled lives of first-year students who posted written entries and photos in eight themed issues a year.

"The bloggers are great admissions recruiters. They know their audience, and their enthusiasm for Bucknell is clear."

Today, A Year in the Life has been converted into a standard blog. The themes have been eliminated and students blog on topics of their choosing.

University staff, faculty members and student interns recommend students whom they think would be great bloggers. Those candidates then complete an application and selection process.

Bloggers are expected to post at least once a week. They are provided with a list of topics from which to choose, if they wish, but are encouraged to write about anything on their minds as long as the material is appropriate and relevant to Bucknell's prospective student audience.

Blogger posts are pending until approved by O'Brien-Foelsch, who reviews them with as light a touch as possible.

"The bloggers are great admissions recruiters," she says. "They know their audience, and their enthusiasm for Bucknell is clear."

Bloggers get to highlight their writing and photography abilities, while demonstrating to prospective employers or graduate schools that they are well-rounded, highly engaged and community-oriented.

How does Bucknell benefit from the student blogs?

"The blogs help prospective students get a feel for the culture of the place, the personalities of the students and the possibilities available to them," says O'Brien-Foelsch. "The project is intended to reach the kind of prospective students Bucknell wants to recruit — those who are passionate about academics and want to have personal connections with their professors."

Source: Molly O'Brien-Foelsch, Senior Writer, Bucknell University, Lewisburg, PA. Phone (570) 577-3260.
E-mail: mobrien@bucknell.edu

23   Avoid These Common Press Release Mistakes

Newsrooms get hundreds of press releases a day. It takes a well-crafted press release to get your nonprofit news coverage. Here are the four biggest press release pitfalls, and guidlines to help you avoid them:

✓ **Burying the lead:** Newsroom decision makers may only have time to can your release. If you don't have an attention-grabbing headline and lead paragraph, you will get overlooked. After that, tell the reporter where to be and when.

✓ **Timing of events:** Most newsroom staffs are lean and most reporters may not report until 9:30 a.m. If you routinely hold events at 8:30 a.m., you may not get coverage.

The same goes for an event that is too late in the day. Know the deadlines for newspaper, television and radio stations in your area and set your events accordingly.

✓ **Providing contact information:** Press contacts and phone numbers should be at the top of your release. Include your office line, cell phone and a second person to contact if you are not available.

✓ **Timing of news releases:** News is a 24/7 business, but most newsrooms are generally staffed from 9:30 a.m. to 10:30 p.m. And your key decision-makers work regular business hours. For that reason, send releases no later than 3 p.m. for next-day events.

24   Advice to Generate and Maximize National News Coverage

Even small nonprofit organizations can gain the attention of national media outlets with a compelling story idea and some serious footwork.

Staff with Amherst College (Amherst, MA) worked for five months to make the college the focus of a June 23, 2009, newspaper article by Bloomberg, which syndicates its stories with 470 newspapers worldwide. The article, Amherst Grads Shun Wall Street, Save World as $45,500 Teachers, highlights the fact that more than half of Amherst's graduating students have committed themselves to working in education or nonprofit sectors. Check it out through this link: www.amherst.edu/taxonomy/term/6987

For Caroline Hanna, director of media relations, and Amherst College President Anthony Marx, the story started in February 2009, when they participated in an editorial board at Bloomberg's headquarters in New York, NY, followed by a few months of personalized e-mail and phone follow-up with several reporters who attended the meeting before one decided to work on this story, Hanna says.

Hanna shares tips on how to make a national media connection:

✓ **Have an important achievement or goal to share.** "Making your message different from others is important. If they can't remember you, why would they want to do a story?"

✓ **Go to an outlet that seems receptive.** Target specific news outlets and their reporters if you don't want your message to get lost. Through social media websites like Facebook (www.facebook.com) and general knowledge of the media organization in question, you can find reporters by name and check out their normal coverage area, as well as what causes they support off the job.

✓ **Initiate and maintain contact through informational meetings.** The critical aspect to engaging a reporter's attention is to not expect a story right away — or even at all. A newspaper editorial board is just one outlet you can pursue. You can also try coffee or a mealtime meeting. "Any kind of relationship with a reporter takes work in a good way, " Hanna says. "It always pays to keep in touch." Also, keep in mind that many newsrooms are understaffed and reporters are juggling a load of stories on tight deadlines. "You can't expect them to drop everything for you," she says.

✓ **Give reporters access to good sources, but also some freedom to explore.** Hanna arranged nearly a full day of on-campus interviews with students and administrators for the Bloomberg reporter. "Having a face-to-face connection is always the best way for them to get a great interview," she says. Allow reporters some open access outside these arrangements to talk to others within your organization — it shows openness and honesty. "You don't want them to feel like you're putting on a big dog-and-pony show, like they're being overly managed," Hanna says.

✓ **Get the word out about the story (when you get it).** Amherst staff posted a link to the Bloomberg story prominently on the college's website for nearly a month and sent the news in the college's bi-weekly e-mail to alumni. Hanna also sent a Twitter message about the story, and linked it to Amherst's Facebook page.

Contact: Caroline Hanna, Director of Media Relations, Amherst College, Amherst, MA. Phone (413) 542-8417.
E-mail: channa@amherst.edu

25   Gearing PR Tools to Your Audience

Identifying the target audience for your next public relations effort can help you create more effective communications vehicles and craft your message to attract those individuals.

Here are some examples:

- **Quarterly magazine or newsletter.** Send these to identified donors, employees, volunteers, board members, key business leaders who have shown interest in your programs, chambers of commerce and news media. This is a valuable tool for keeping constituents informed, and to those who can continue to call attention to your services.

- **The Internet and e-mail.** Busy professionals and volunteers often rely on laptops and electronic devices to keep them in touch with the world. Your website, online or PDF format newsletter and e-mail announcements will keep them in the loop. A Midwestern university recently notified students that they had been accepted using text messaging in addition to formal letters.

- **Targeted direct mail advertising.** When you have a broad audience to reach in a specific area, contact a direct mail house for ZIP-coded prospects narrowed

to demographics you seek. Some can also produce the postcards and handle the mailing. Potential clients in your area will learn about services and programs that will be convenient for them to access.

- **Brochures and flyers.** Who will be most interested in the activity or service you want to promote? Keep in mind the age of the audience and tailor graphics and copy accordingly. Teen volunteers may be attracted to brighter ink and paper colors, while donors and board members who may be older may be more responsive to a straightforward approach with more detailed information.

- **Radio and television.** The public service announcements you have taped to air during the morning drive radio market reports will have different listeners than the Top 40 pop station playing at the coffee shop in the late afternoon. Consider using different voices and background music that are appropriate for the audience and time of day, even if the message is nearly the same. Think of the differences between CNN and MTV when choosing where to run your commercials, placing them where they are most likely to be noticed.

26   Crafting Then-and-now Stories For Maximum Effect

Then-and-now stories can show longevity, stability and growth.

In addition, staff with the Make-A-Wish Foundation of Northeast New York (Cohoes, NY) learned that comparing where your organization (or a client or a staff person or a program) has been and where it is today can clarify your mission.

Dogged by the misperception that all the children Make-A-Wish serves are terminally ill, the communications staff decided then-and-now stories were the perfect way to show that persons who had their wishes granted 10, 15 or even 20 years ago were still alive and thriving.

The concept was a huge success, with more than 20 former wish children acting as ambassadors at events and appearing in feature stories in media outlets throughout the foundation's territory.

The following tips were used by foundation staff to ensure the effort met with success:

- ❏ **Start early.** This gives you time to follow up with as many respondents as possible, guaranteeing the most compelling stories. You may also need time to locate

certain people who have lost contact over the years.

- ❏ **Have a point.** Create a theme to tie stories together and drive a certain message home. Maybe your hospital is about to install cutting edge research equipment and you're planning a capital campaign. Showing donors how far you have come can encourage them to invest in how far you can go.

- ❏ **Flesh out subjects.** Allow potential subjects to talk about who they are now as a whole, not just in relation to your organization. Doing so will help you target additional media outlets.

- ❏ **Make the numbers.** If planning a major media or fund-raising campaign based on then-and-now stories, make sure you have enough stories to keep the campaign fresh. Editors want new information, or at the very least, a new angle. Using the same story over and over again in your own publications can also turn people off.

- ❏ **Get the picture.** Include visual images from the past and today with any pitch for a then-and-now story.

27 Photo Tour Showcases New Addition

Spotlight your new or enhanced facility with an online photo tour like the one used by Covenant Hospice (Pensacola, FL) to promote a building addition.

"Warm brownies, birthday parties, family gatherings, and places for family to bond are all unexpected sites at the residence," says Don Ruth, director of communications. To encourage persons to make in-person visits and experience the site firsthand, Ruth says, they promoted an online photo tour showcasing the facility's warm, inviting atmosphere.

During the addition's construction, Melissa Chapman, multimedia specialist, conducted two 30-minute photo shoots to document the progress and collect images for the photo tour. She utilized the photo album features built into the hospice's content management system, called Tendenci, to create the tour.

"Because we are a nonprofit, it was not feasible to purchase video equipment or hardware to create professional panoramic tours," says Chapman. "With basic photography equipment and Web tools, we are able to update patients, families, donors and the community as to the progress of our new addition in ways that a written description can't convey."

They notified donors by direct mail about the addition and invited them to take the online and in-person tours.

Chapman cites one unexpected perk of the online feature: Persons attending open houses "were excited to be able to go back home and show additional family members what they got to see" by logging on to the online photo tour.

Sources: Don Ruth, Director of Communications; Melissa Chapman, Multimedia Specialist; Covenant Hospice, Pensacola, FL. Phone (850) 433-2155.

28 Campus-wide Theme Heralds New Goals for College

An appropriate theme for your next special event or capital campaign can act as a catalyst to spread the news through and beyond your intended audience.

In celebration of the inauguration of their eighth president, staff at Scripps College (Claremont, CA) selected a unique, campus-wide theme: The Genius of Women. The theme is intended to engage students and faculty in discussions on why creative and intellectual genius is essential in today's changing world, especially from women for women, says Steve Sabicer, public relations director.

Such themes, Sabicer says, "create a personality for the communications objective, and in the case of an inauguration or leadership change, can foreshadow the goals and objectives the new executive or leader wants to achieve in their role."

In addition, the public relations director says, benefits of overall themes include:

- **Clarity of message:** The theme is a reference point and message platform from which all materials and communications should be drawn, providing continuity and connection to the communication objective.

- **Synergy with other milestones:** Scripps staff found that the theme could be applied to many events and milestones on campus that originally were not considered part of the inauguration. "The theme was broad enough," says Sabicer, "and also relevant enough, to be adopted by other functions and groups on campus that might not have participated in the original campaign. It would have been hard to achieve that sense of community without a theme."

Theme's Unexpected Perk: Students, Faculty Make It Their Own

Take the time up front to brainstorm a great theme or catch phrase for your next campaign, and you may just find it takes on a life of its own, spreading positive publicity beyond your hoped-for expectations.

Steve Sabicer, public relations director, Scripps College (Claremont, CA) says their campus-wide theme, The Genius of Women, has had an additional benefit they did not expect when they were in the planning stages:

"Our students and faculty have actually co-opted the theme for their own purposes, and developed creative ways to describe what The Genius of Women means to them (art projects and curriculum changes), which we embrace wholeheartedly. It ensures the theme gains visibility in communities that may get their information from more selective sources or that may disregard more conventional channels for communication."

- **Global voice:** A theme provides an easy way to address larger global issues, and it grabs the audience's attention when they may have simply overlooked the facts. Sabicer says, "In our sound bite culture, everyone is looking for the 10-second summary. A theme helps us provide that for bigger issues."

Source: Steve Sabicer, Director, Public Relations, Scripps College, Claremont, CA. Phone (909) 607-9665.
E-mail: SSabicer@scrippscollege.edu.

29 Gain Public Approval by Connecting With Other Local Nonprofits

Consider collaborating with other nonprofits in your community to share event expenses, enhance community awareness or gain positive visibility.

Officials with Brazosport College (Lake Jackson, TX) decided to promote the renovation of a campus jogging trail with the help of several community organizations, including two nonprofits. The collaboration joined the college with Brazosport Running Club; SPCA (Society for the Prevention of Cruelty to Animals) of Brazoria County; the cities of Lake Jackson, Richwood, Clute and Freeport; a family fitness club; and the Brazosport Regional Health System.

The partnership with other community organizations helped relay the message that the trail is not just for the college's benefit, but for the benefit of the entire community, says Patty Sayes, director of public information and communications.

To help celebrate the trail reopening, Sayes says, the SPCA hosted a pet parade that helped draw traffic and publicity to the rededication festivities, as well as lead to adoption of some of the shelter's cats and dogs.

The Brazosport Running Club assisted in adding mile markers to the trail and promoting the event to its club members, Sayes adds, while the college used the event as a prime opportunity to promote the club and their events.

Source: Patty Sayes, Director of Public Information and Communications, Brazosport College, Lake Jackson, TX. Phone (979) 230-3241. E-mail: patty.sayes@brazosport.edu

30 Photo Contest Engages Constituents, Introduces New Mascot

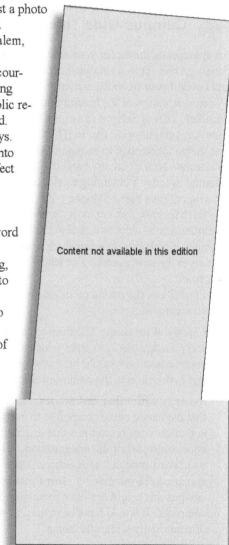

Content not available in this edition

Looking to promote your brand, engage your constituents and generate buzz? Host a photo contest in which your mascot or other highly recognizable icon takes center stage.

That was the tactic taken by the public relations team at Roanoke College (Salem, VA) when the college launched a new mascot — Rooney, a maroon-tailed hawk.

In the first-ever Little Rooney Spring Break Photo Contest, students were encouraged to take Little Rooney (a plush doll of the college's new mascot) on their spring break travels and photograph his adventures, says Teresa Gereaux, director of public relations. Students could submit the images for a chance to win a bookstore gift card.

"We literally laughed out loud when we saw some of the pictures," Gereaux says. "Rooney underwater. Rooney with Donald Duck. Rooney sending a hello squawk into outer space from a telescope in Puerto Rico. It was just funny and silly, and the perfect way to increase visibility of our new mascot."

Gereaux says three goals drove the contest: 1) to promote awareness of and interaction with the new mascot; 2) to enable students, faculty and staff to create content that would tie in to Roanoke's brand; and 3) to generate excitement and word of mouth.

They announced the contest to the student body by e-mail, on the college blog, and in the campus bookstore with posters and displays. They posted submissions to Facebook (www.facebook.com) as they were received.

Gereaux says winning images were not only creative and humorous, they also showed the student body's spring break activities — from a Habitat for Humanity project in New Orleans and volunteer work in Nicaragua, to skiing on the slopes of Vermont and deep-sea diving in St. Croix.

"We always try to communicate some of the interesting things our students are doing over spring break, whether it's in a blog post or something like that," Gereaux says. "This was a little bit different way, a more fun way, to do that and also accomplish some of our larger goals."

Source: Teresa Gereaux, Director of Public Relations, Roanoke College, Salem, VA. Phone (540) 375-2282. E-mail: gereaux@roanoke.edu Website: www.roanoke.edu

Submissions to the 2010 Little Rooney Spring Break contest included Little Rooney taking to the slopes at Vermont's Mount Snow, top, and Rooney eating at Cafe du Monde in New Orleans, LA. For more examples of how Roanoke College students and faculty shared their spring break with the new mascot, go to http://roanoke.edu/About_Roanoke/Traditions/Rooney.htm and click on the link, "Little Rooney Photo Contest."

31   Three Ways to Make the Most of Letters to the Editor

A letter to the editor of your local, regional or even a national newspaper or magazine is a simple way to raise awareness about your organization.

But this tried-and-tested communications method can be so much more than an awareness raiser. These ideas can help you make the most of your next letter to the editor:

1. **Have a point.** Using a letter to the editor to thank the community for their support of a fundraiser or event is OK, though it's important to make it relevant. Tie the need for your organization to current events. Include recently updated statistics that relate to your work or a timely issue that your organization is helping to address.

2. **Be an expert.** Use your knowledge and role to educate others about the headlines. Writing a letter offering more detailed information or advice about breaking news stories still gets your organization out there, while serving the community as a whole. It may even lead to additional exposure if local reporters start to view you as an expert on specific subjects.

3. **Offer assistance.** If your organization provides assistance that can help people with a problem existing in your community, make sure to let them know that. Be the solution people can find in an unlikely place.

Whether written by yourself, your CEO/executive director, your board president or even a satisfied employee or client, keep the letter to the editor brief and memorable. Written well, a letter to the editor can be a powerful tool to help further your goals.

32   Centennial Timeline Returns College to Founding Principles

When staff and faculty at Reed College (Portland, OR) began considering options for marking the college's centennial anniversary that will take place in 2011, they outlined a number of different projects designed to help the Reed community appropriately celebrate and preserve the institution's history.

One idea that is proving to be most useful and popular is an interactive centennial timeline, displayed prominently on the college's website.

Jennifer Bates, director of public affairs, says the timeline not only informs their audience of the college's goals, mission and history, it creates a lasting digital archive of the items in the school's special collections.

The visually driven timeline has been a hit among the many college audiences, Bates says: "People seem to enjoy the site and like being able to learn about and see images from our founding years. They also enjoy learning that the college is still true to its founding principles."

While it has been a success, Bates says it required a significant amount of work. A subcommittee worked with an outside design firm to make the timeline a reality. Sections and topics were determined by that committee, with the actual narrative being written by alumnus. Special collections and public affairs worked closely together to edit, organize and post the content.

In the end, the timeline ended up being a two-phase project. The current site that focuses on the college's founding years was launched in January 2009 in preparation for the start of the college's centennial campaign. The second phase of the website will launch in January 2011 to coincide with their centennial year.

Bates says dividing the timeline into two distinct projects helped with the workload. "By choosing to focus on the first few years of the college for this first site, we significantly reduced the amount of content. We focused on telling the institution's story, and included as many of the supporting documents we could find."

See Reed College's centennial timeline at: http://centennial.reed.edu/

Source: Jennifer Bates, Director of Public Affairs, Reed College, Portland, OR.
Phone (503) 777-7289. E-mail: jennifer.bates@reed.edu.
Website: http://centennial.reed.edu/

Make Time for Challenges When Creating Timeline

Creating a project such as an interactive online 100-year timeline can be especially challenging because the project is so new and labor-intensive.

But that didn't stop officials at Reed College (Portland, OR), who created such a timeline in anticipation of the college's 100th anniversary in 2011. See the interactive timeline at: http://centennial.reed.edu/

Jennifer Bates, director of public affairs, says the two most significant challenges of the centennial project were: 1) outlining the framework for the first phase of the timeline while keeping the second phase in mind; and 2) presenting information to two very divergent audiences — the Reed community, which is very familiar with the institution, and an external audience that may know very little about Reed.

How did they overcome those challenges? Communication.

Bates says Reed officials held many meetings to discuss the challenges and ways to overcome them.

Another important factor, she says, was allowing a great deal of lead time for discussions and implementations.

33 Rule of Thumb

Choosing the Right Media — Selecting the right media for your message can be challenging, so keep this in mind: The more important the message, the more personally it should be delivered.

Putting a human presence with a message through direct interaction dramatically increases its impact. On the other hand, blanketing a wide audience with a general advertisement relies on the sheer number of viewers or listeners.

34 Land in the Spotlight When the Media Comes to Town

No matter what the size of your community, news media will be attracted to either scheduled or unannounced special events in your city. Examples include visits from political or entertainment personalities, seasonal sports activities or popular annual festivals.

As a representative of your organization, you may see logical and tasteful opportunities to promote your cause when media representatives are expected on the scene. Being in the right place at the right time with the right motivation requires a balance of intuition and readiness if you are to gain positive exposure for your institution.

Here are strategies to put your organization's media readiness mechanism in place for both expected and un-planned events:

❑ **Look for seasonal opportunities.** During state or national election years, realize that national political leaders may be visiting your area to support a local or regional candidate. Most of these possible visits will be during the weeks prior to a spring primary, or before November elections. Contacts your congressman's and senator's staffs in Washington, or at the local level. Keep these influential persons informed of your valuable programs, especially those that may replace a government-funded service. Let them know your facility is open to them when they are in the area, knowing that they will be seeking photo opportunities for their own images — touring your facility could be one of them.

❑ **Remember the sports fans.** Even small communities will have sports teams at the high school or college level. Their regular games may be the most newsworthy events for a majority of the year. If they are having a winning season, media coverage will increase as they near tournament finals. Having a mutually beneficial partnership with an appropriate sports team in your community can increase your own coverage and may be a story in itself.

❑ **Be a sponsor of crowd-pleasing events.** Even if your hands are full handling your own programs, you may offer to be an outlet for ticket sales, use your printing press to run some flyers, and offer various levels of cooperation to help ensure the events' success. Offer to reward your most loyal volunteers with tickets your organization has purchased for them, and encourage them to wear apparel such as hats or T-shirts with your logo. Photographers are likely to notice groups of people dressed similarly to promote a worthwhile organization, and even ask them why they are there.

Being in the right place at the right time with the right motivation requires a balance of intuition and readiness if you are to gain positive exposure for your institution.

❑ **Think of your city's famous natives.** Even if you aren't located in the birthplace of Clint Eastwood, Madonna or other celebrity types, chances are there are some well-known individuals from your area who may return home for one reason or another. Learn about their favorite causes and look for a link to one of your programs. If they won't come specifically to raise funds or increase awareness of your organization, they may be open to visiting if they happen to be in the area for personal reasons.

❑ **Ask your supporters for assistance.** If you invite your local newspaper editor to be on your board of directors or community advisory committee, you have a reason to send him or her regular progress reports. Finding media representatives who believe in your mission and inviting them to be among your leaders (if it isn't a professional conflict of interest) may help increase your exposure simply because they are regularly informed of your activities.

❑ **Have current press kits ready at all times.** Sometimes negative circumstances bring news crews to your community, such as weather disasters or transportation accidents. Being a good citizen and rallying your organization's supporters to help others will be a positive note for media to find during a difficult story. The benefits are maximized when you are performing a truly needed service in an emergency, and showing your community spirit. Have general information about your programs in folders and ready to distribute if asked by busy reporters.

35 Publicize Volunteer Efforts

Publicize your organization's volunteers and volunteer programs not just because they deserve the spotlight, but because doing so helps spread the word about your programs and services.

To gain media exposure, honor supporters and find new sources of volunteers:

✓ **Spotlight existing corporate partnerships.** Write news releases about the company's good citizenship ties with your organization and community enhancement goals.

✓ **Create a video.** Have key volunteers share their feelings about helping your institution on camera. Include a variety of people using the remarks that best make your point. Use the video to recruit, in PSAs and prospect presentations.

✓ **Celebrate National Volunteer Week.** Use this annual celebration, held each April, to spotlight your hard workers and volunteer opportunities, contacting the news media as early as January to express interest in being included in feature articles or advertising supplements and to suggest names of volunteers who would make good feature stories.

✓ **Be innovative and imaginative.** Even if you have a small promotion budget, create posters to put in neighborhood supermarkets or shops with a lighthearted theme such as "WANTED: More Volunteers Like Mary Smith" using Mary's photo, a few words about her efforts for your cause, and where newcomers can join.

✓ **Look for good news stories.** Seek out stories about relationships between your volunteers and the people they help. Encourage news reporters to speak to the subjects themselves, after you have made introductions.

✓ **Watch for benchmarks.** Are your volunteers about to prepare the 10,000th meal for shut-ins, mark the 100,000th hour reading to the visually disabled, or give the 30,000th toy to a child at Christmas? Plan for the arrival of these milestones with a small event or ceremony that can be photographed or covered by the media and featured in your organization's newsletter. This type of coverage recognizes both volunteers and your organization's good deeds.

36 Add Facebook Cause Page to Your Communications Options

Social networking is here to stay. However, the options can be a bit overwhelming.

One popular venue is Facebook (www.facebook.com), which offers pages for individuals as well as sites where people can join your group or cause.

All nonprofits should create a cause page on Facebook, advises JoAnn McKenzie, social media instructor, Northeast Community College (Norfolk, NE).

A Facebook cause page allows 501(c)(3) nonprofit organizations to solicit online donations, significantly boosting an organization's fundraising potential and extending an organization's reach as far as the Internet can go. Also, Facebook cause pages typically receive more visits than does an organization's home page.

According to McKenzie, the process to set up a cause page is simple and allows multiple people to serve as page administrators. Before you can begin using the page for online donations, you need to fill out forms to verify your 501(c)(3) nonprofit status.

Once you have created your cause page, she says, have your staff, board members and volunteers sign up as fans or friends of your page and encourage them to spread the word to all their friends, both through Facebook and other means.

Additional benefits of a Facebook cause page? Access

> **Tips for Creating Facebook Cause Page**
>
> When creating a cause page on Facebook (www.facebook.com) for your organization, be sure to control your message, advises JoAnn McKenzie, social media instructor, Northeast Community College (Norfolk, NE).
>
> McKenzie suggests having two to three key people in your organization assigned to monitor the cause page. Page administrators need to make sure the page is continually evolving and engaging your volunteers and donor base, and they must remove inappropriate or immature comments posted to your site.
>
> Also, be wary of downloading or accessing any applications. According to McKenzie, while a Facebook application may seem like fun, some of them can allow your computer to be the target for spam or spyware.

to Facebook's group and fan pages and the ability to share educational information, recruit volunteers, advertise special events and share news about your cause.

Source: JoAnn McKenzie, Adjunct Faculty, Northeast Community College, Norfolk, NE. Phone (402) 369-0804.
E-mail: joann@northeast.edu

37 Properly Stock Your Press Conference Toolkit

You've sent your news releases and the big day has arrived. Do you have what you need to make the event a success?

Follow this checklist and you will.

❑ **Press packets** including a copy of your news release, a list of who will be speaking with their contact information and correct spelling of their names, a general brochure or fact sheet about your organization and a style guide about writing for your organization.

❑ **Extra copies of news releases** for reporters who don't want to bother with a whole packet of info. Having a few extra releases to hand to them will prevent you from having to sort through the packets to pull one out.

❑ **Business cards** to give to people for follow-up.

❑ **An attendee sign-in sheet** to help you follow up with attendees.

❑ **A greeter** to welcome people as they arrive. Ask them to fill out the sign-in sheet and hand them a press packet, freeing you to answer questions and mingle.

❑ **Technical support**, or the person who knows how to use the microphone, laptop or other equipment necessary for the conference to go off without a hitch.

❑ **Key constituents** who commit their time or money to you, plus a few people who have benefited from your services. Clarify their roles for them and limit the number you invite so it doesn't get overwhelming for attendees.

❑ **Light refreshments** that encourage people to linger and get more information after the formal program.

❑ **Miscellaneous needs,** such as tissues, gum, mints, extra pens, note pads, etc. to address those just-in-case emergencies.

❑ **Additional literature** to be taken by any interested attendee.

38 Maximize Your Message on Twitter In 140 Characters or Less

A nonprofit's Twitter account can be a gold mine for fundraising, volunteer outreach, marketing and publicity. The trick is figuring out how to best communicate your organization's purpose and needs in Twitspeak.

For example, one rule of Twitter is that each tweet (electronic message to persons who sign up to follow you) can contain no more than 140 characters of type, including punctuation and spaces. So what can you convey in such a short space that can result in a positive change in your organization's bottom line, membership base or press coverage?

Jennifer Roccanti, development associate at Miriam's Kitchen, a Washington, D.C.-based provider of meals and essential services for the homeless, uses Twitter daily.

"We've found that people genuinely want to make a difference in the lives of our guests," says Roccanti, "and Twitter is one way we can connect our supporters to ways they can help." Here are her recommendations for tweeting to your best advantage.

Use recurring headers. Many Miriam's Kitchen tweets begin "One Thing You Can Do Today To Help," and then suggest something inspirational ("Give thanks for the people in your life") or ask for something ("Can you spare a warm hat for a person on the street?"). Other tweets start with "On the Menu This Morning," listing what Miriam's Kitchen will serve guests that day, allowing people to feel connected to Miriam's Kitchen on a daily basis. But the tweets that generate the most results are those that begin, "On Our Wish List Today." Which is why Roccanti most recommends that you...

Tweet for in-kind donations. More than fundraising, Twitter has proven to be a gold mine for Miriam's Kitchen when in need of specific items. Roccanti might ask for something like, "Men's jeans, especially sizes 34 and 36." "We try to be as specific as possible and mention things that really anyone could do," she says. "We want to give our supporters a quick way to get involved, and they've really responded. In fact, I just got a huge box of books from one of our friends on Twitter."

Get personal. "Our most popular tweets are ones about our guests or the struggles they are facing," says Roccanti. "Statistics about homelessness, stories about our guests or links to articles about the issue at large are usually retweeted." Retweets (when a user forwards your tweets to his or her own followers) are an easy and effective way to expand your potential base of donors and members and to spread your message far and wide — with others doing the work for you.

Jennifer Roccanti, Development Associate, Miriam's Kitchen, Washington, D.C. Phone (202) 452-8926. E-mail: jenn@miriamskitchen.org

39 Cater E-newsletter Content to Target Audiences

Q. How do you target various audiences to get your message out?

"One way is through e-newsletters. Calvin College (Grand Rapids, MI) has four — Calvin Wire, which offers breaking news and alumni updates; Calvin-Parents (for parents of students); Calvin-Sports Report (featuring the latest on college athletes); and Calvin-Connection, which has information about on-campus programs and events open to the public. This allows us to send our message directly to our constituents, while reaching very distinct audiences. We determined it would be more widely read if the publications were specific to the audience.

"We are also able to inform and remind neighbors and friends about learning opportunities at or sponsored by Calvin and increase attendance at these events, while allowing us to promote photo galleries and video, too.

"Feedback has been mostly positive. We get a lot of thank yous and many people stay on the lists long after their child has graduated.

"Our distribution frequency varies from twice a month with Calvin Wire to daily for Calvin-Sports Report, with each publication going out to anywhere from 500 (Calvin-Connection) to 6,527 recipients (Calvin-Parents)."

Source: Lynn Rosendale, Associate Director Communications and Marketing, Calvin College, Grand Rapids, MI.
Phone (616) 526-6861. E-mail: lrosenda@calvin.edu

40 Year in Review Can Boost Morale, Show Value

In large organizations, there is always a lot going on — much of it newsworthy. To help recap and focus that positive coverage, compile a year-in-review feature that you share on your website and/or in print form.

Nicole Pitaniello, assistant vice president for public relations, Albany Medical Center (Albany, NY) says its year-in-review piece is a source of pride for the organization. The piece, she says, reminds people of the great things that happened at the center over the year while underscoring how valuable their publicity is to the institution.

"People sometimes comment that we don't do enough paid advertising," Pitaniello says. "The year-in-review feature is a way to help offset that argument. We are able to show that the communications department yields benefits for the hospital.

"By placing these in-depth stories in a variety of local media, we're getting way more space and credibility than we could ever afford through traditional advertising. We're getting double and triple the coverage this way. We're also getting third-party credibility because it's an outside source saying the work we do is valued. It's not just coming from us."

In addition, Pitaniello says, "It's a nice reminder for people to keep us in the loop about what is happening, so we have the stories to tell."

Source: Nicole Pitaniello, Assistant Vice President for Public Relations, Albany Medical Center, Albany, NY.
Phone (518) 262-3421. E-mail: PitaniN@ mail.amc.edu.
Website: http://www.amc.edu/pr/yearinreview/year_in_review.html

41 Use Editorials to Further Your Cause

Newspaper editorials represent one way to grab the attention of the public. By selectively and thoughtfully responding to current issues in this venue, you and key constituents can bring about positive attention to your cause and highlight its worthiness for support.

Whether your CEO, a board member or a friendly constituent offers an occasional editorial that casts a favorable light on your cause, these public opinions provide a subtle but widespread way of enhancing your organizational image in the minds of readers.

While it's important not to overuse this technique so as to avoid appearing contrived, here are some general topics that might call for editorials:

- A message of congratulations from a supporter when your organization has just completed a successful event, program or community service project.

- An opinion on how your organization is positively addressing a current issue with local, regional or national importance.

- A statement on ways in which your cause positively impacts the community, economically and culturally.

Be Sure Your Story Gets Heard

You have a great story. You've crafted the perfect release. You send it, then sit back and hope it doesn't end up as a coaster for some beat reporter's coffee cup.

How can you make sure your news release gets printed or on the airwaves?

Michael Schwartzberg, media relations manager, Greater Baltimore Medical Center (Baltimore, MD) and former journalist, shares a few sure-fire ways to do so:

✓ **Get involved.** Schwartzberg says he is an active member on the board of the Baltimore Public Relations Council. As a result, he benefits from the organization's listserv of changes in the local media and the programs they offer dealing with local news outlets and their personnel.

✓ **Get informed.** Schwartzberg actively follows the local news, reading the local daily and weekly papers and watching the newscasts of all four networks. This allows him to stay on top of who is coming and going, along with who is covering what.

✓ **Get concise.** Try sending news releases via e-mail with only the most compelling paragraph in the body. Attach the full text (unless you know certain outlets automatically send attachments to the junk bin) and include a link to the full text on your organization's website.

✓ **Get targeted.** One way Schwartzberg targets distribution to appeal to the largest number of outlets is to make sure his sources are from several geographic areas, increasing the interest of smaller, community-based outlets. He says he also makes a point of considering if a particular story is better for a print outlet or a broadcast outlet (great visuals or interview potential).

Source: Michael Schwartzberg, Media Relations Manager, Greater Baltimore Medical Center, Baltimore, MD. Phone (443) 849-2126. E-mail: mschwartzberg@gbmc.org

 Radio Helps the Public Tune Into Your Events

How many times a day do you listen to a radio? Whether at home, in the car, at the office or in a shopping mall, you're likely to hear news or music from a local radio station.

Most radio stations support local charitable causes in the form of public service announcements (PSAs), station personalities appearing at fundraising events and even doing remote broadcasts. Many even co-sponsor events with organizations.

Enlisting the support of one or more local radio stations can be a tremendous advantage in increasing community awareness of your efforts and interesting new donors in contributing to your cause. Begin by identifying which station's music or broadcast format is best suited to your target audience.

The Arbitron Company (www.arbitron.com) researches and measures radio audiences in hundreds of local markets, identifying which stations, programs and times of day various age groups and genders are listening to a particular station. Companies use these results to determine how much air time they will buy from various stations and at which times of day they are most likely to reach target groups.

Being aware of who is listening to the radio stations in your area will help concentrate your efforts on the station with the greatest number of listeners who fit your demographics.

When you have determined which stations to approach for assistance, prepare a proposal, which may include any of the following requests:

• **Brief appearances by you or your event chairs.** Ask to be a guest on a morning or afternoon news program where you can spend a few minutes telling listeners about your event and its purpose. Include information and phone numbers for tickets and times. Some radio stations will agree to be a ticket outlet as well.

• **Celebrity appearances by station personalities.** Most radio stations send their personalities to the site of the event to do brief updates about the success of the event, and encourage others to join the festivities.

• **Public service announcements.** These are like free 10-, 15- or 30-second commercials about your event. Free airtime may be at a premium since many organizations make such requests, but it's worth attempting.

• **Sponsorship of a major event.** Such a request usually requires many months or even a year of advance planning, as many radio stations are committed far in advance. Think of ways the station will benefit from an association with your organization, offering major recognition status in any publicity you receive from other media as well. But remember that competitive stations will not be likely to offer their support at the same time.

Approach station managers and news personnel as you would a major sponsor. You will have plenty of competition from other organizations that recognize the priceless value of positive exposure on that station. Offering to pay for some commercials during peak rate time may result in additional free time during slower programming hours.

44 Negotiations, Flexibility Maximize Use of Billboard Advertising

What's a good way to reach a target audience at the most reasonable cost?

As nonprofit representatives puzzle over that question, they often overlook outdoor ads — billboards in particular — as being too expensive, complicated or ineffective.

But when officials with the national nonprofit agency, Suicide Awareness Voices of Education (SAVE), Minneapolis, MN, wanted to take a public health approach to increasing awareness that suicide was preventable, and they thought billboards would be a good way to do it, says Dan Reidenberg, executive director.

"It was a way to reach large numbers with a small budget in a short amount of time," Reidenberg says.

Working originally with Wisconsin ad agency Goltz Seering, and more recently the Minneapolis-based agency Nemer-Fieger, SAVE officials developed simple, high impact art and copy, and contacted billboard companies to discuss placement costs.

Negotiating billboard production and display costs is a way for nonprofits to get more mileage out of their advertising dollar. Reidenberg notes that billboard companies may be open to negotiating costs, especially when posting signs for nonprofit agencies. For example, SAVE has offered to pay for one month in exchange for a month free (or running in five additional areas for free). Billboard companies produced the boards on paper or reusable vinyl and stored them in their warehouse until space was available that SAVE could use.

SAVE officials, in partnership with the University of Minnesota's Department of Psychiatry, conducted research on the use of billboards in social marketing campaigns. The results indicated that thoroughly pre-testing the message was important for safe and effective messaging campaigns, Reidenberg notes. Calls, letters and e-mails to the agency also suggest that placement of the billboards in suburban areas rather than major highways is an important consideration.

Results of the billboard campaign are tracked by the number of in-state calls and out-of-state calls that mention the campaign.

These billboards by Suicide Awareness Voices of Education (Minneapolis, MN) are running nationwide to build a culture of change about mental illness and suicide prevention.

Dan Reidenberg, Executive Director, Suicide Awareness Voices of Education, Minneapolis, MN. Phone (952) 946-7998. E-mail: dreidenberg@save.org

45 Appreciation Activities Build Goodwill, Publicity

Offering clients, volunteers or supporters a thank-you gift — while expecting nothing in return — helps strengthen loyalty and goodwill that will inevitably pay back through word-of-mouth publicity.

Here are ideas for doing so:

✓ **Give a custom gift basket.** Contact them by phone, postcard or e-mail to give them a choice of items such as gourmet coffee, chocolates, nuts or sugar-free candy, sparkling cider or champagne, plus tickets to an upcoming event or free admission to your facilities for themselves and a friend.

✓ **Host a spa escape.** Hire professionals with portable massage chairs or tables, manicure stations, facials or foot rubs. Include services that appeal to both genders and all ages. Offer light and healthy refreshments like calming teas, savory salads and whole grain breads.

Choose a relaxing venue such as a large atrium with natural light, running water and plants. Send gift certificates to those who are not able to attend.

✓ **Offer professional lessons.** Buy a group of your most dedicated supporters an hour-long session with their choice of a makeup artist, wardrobe consultant, golf pro, investment consultant or home staging professional. Look for experts who appeal to almost everyone in your database.

✓ **Plan a brunch and photo event.** Invite clients/donors and families for Sunday brunch at a hotel or banquet facility, followed by a photo session for the family, individuals or even a baby. Give them one photo as a gift — in a frame with your logo — and the option to purchase more from the photographer.

46 Tell Your Organization's Story Through Photos

Use images of your facilities, people and programs to tell the story of your cause.

In March 2008, staff with the University of San Francisco (USF) of San Francisco, CA, created a 61-photo "day in the life" slideshow for USF's print and online magazines.

"This was a fun way for our readers to experience a 'slice of life' on campus," says Angie Davis, director of communications, USF School of Law and former editor of USF Magazine. "Many of our 80,000 readers, who are primarily alumni, haven't visited campus recently. We wanted to convey the vibrancy of our campus community, the diversity of our people and programs, how our mission is lived out on a daily basis, and just what it's like to spend a day on campus."

Two freelance photographers and one in-house photographer shot the images, taking a combined 1,400 photos in one day.

"We negotiated a standard full-day rate that included print and Web use of the photos," says Davis.

Planning which areas of campus would be photographed and at what times took roughly one month to coordinate. Doing so involved steps such as working with professors whose classes they wanted to photograph in action and determining where landscapers would be planting trees that day.

"I came up with a rough schedule of events and activities including classes, sporting events, lectures and

rehearsals that were scheduled on the photo day, and I split up the assignments among the photographers," says Davis. "I also built in plenty of time for them to explore and roam the campus to capture the unplanned, spontaneous moments.

"Once the photos came back, I worked with our in-house team of four graphic designers to choose which photos to include in the magazine."

They shared the finished product in print and electronic versions of the magazine and on USF's intranet. Some photos shot during the day have been used in admissions brochures.

"We received very positive feedback from the campus community and readers, who said (the 'day in the life' feature) gave them a vivid picture of life at USF," says Davis. "One staff member told me it reminded him of why he is so proud to be a part of this university."

For organizations thinking of creating a photo story, Davis offers this advice: "The key is finding the right balance between having enough scheduled activities and events, and allowing enough free time for the photographers to use their own instincts in capturing spontaneous moments. I would recommend using photographers whose strength is in photojournalism."

Source: Angie Davis, Director of Communications, University of San Francisco, School of Law, San Francisco, CA. Phone (415) 422-4409.

47 Make Employee Profiles More Than Just Profiles

When crafting your next employee profile, don't just switch to autopilot. Rather, look for ways to wow your readers and create a piece that does more than fill the white space.

At the Worcester, MA, chapter of Dismas House, a nonprofit that provides transitional housing and support services to former prison inmates, Dave McMahon, co-executive director, uses employee profiles he writes to enhance grant submissions and funder proposals. On occasion, he expands a profile to make it the centerpiece of an annual appeal. He has even submitted pieces for competition, noting that a profile on Dismas House co-director Colleen Hilferty recently won a Bank of America Local Hero award.

To get more out of employee profiles, McMahon says, write less. He suggests one concise paragraph with a list of key accomplishments, years in the field and any standout innovative practices.

But remember that less doesn't mean modest.

"Start off with a bang, attracting the reader to a really headline accomplishment," says McMahon, especially when it comes to potential donors. "It will get tossed instantly unless something really grabs a funder's attention in the first line, such as 'Harvard fellow,' or 'top seven in the country.' The most unique attribute about each staff member should be in the introduction."

McMahon's award-winning Hilferty profile began with: "Under Colleen's leadership, Dismas was selected as one of the top seven prisoner re-entry programs nationally by the Eisenhower Institute." After that eye-catching lead, says McMahon, "then backfill with how many years he or she has been with the agency, other experience and an educational profile or awards."

Just like a resume, he says, a profile should stick to professional achievements. "A funder doesn't want to know about your kids or hobbies, they want to see competence, results and something fresh and unique. Save the other stuff for Facebook."

An exception to this would be if one employee engages in community-based, unpaid work relevant to your organization's mission, such as work on election campaigns or with other nonprofits' boards. "A staff member of mine was just named to the board of a local health center," he says. "You can bet that it will appear in his staff profile in the first line, followed by his story as a former prisoner who turned his life around."

Source: Dave McMahon, Co-Executive Director, Dismas House, Worcester, MA. Phone (508) 767-9389.
E-mail: davemcmahon@dismashouse.org.
Website: www.dismashouse.org

48 Tips on Delivering Bad News

Nobody wants to announce offices are closing or a popular program is being cut, but sometimes it has to be done.

Kivi Miller, president of Nonprofit Marketing Guide.com and author of "The Nonprofit Marketing Guide: High-Impact, Low-Cost Ways to Build Support for Your Good Cause," shares advice for delivering bad news while inflicting minimal damage to stakeholder relationships.

When sharing bad news, Miller says, "Always be completely honest and transparent. Don't try to cover up or gloss over unpopular aspects of the news. But also be sure to focus on the positive results that will come from the news or event. Find some kind of silver lining and make that the heart of your message.

"Those who are the most impacted or who will have the strongest opinions — the board of directors or major donors — should be notified first and well before the news goes public," she says. "Stakeholders who will be heavily affected — the parents of children attending a daycare that will be closing, for example — should also be given plenty of advance notice. One exception is if you are working to find an alternative to offer. Then it's better to wait to have some good news to deliver with the bad."

If you need to acknowledge culpability or guilt, Miller says, have persons who have the ultimate responsibility for resolving the problem do the talking. Have them address not just the incident itself but steps you have taken to prevent similar situations from happening again. Couple long-term solutions to immediate problems.

Lastly, Miller says, when it comes to sharing bad news, "There is a very fine balance between not sharing enough detail and sharing too much. On one side, if you share bad news but don't explain what happened in sufficient detail, people's imaginations will fill in the gaps, and that will almost always be worse than what really happened. On the other side, people don't need a blow-by-blow of who said what when or a rundown of the reactions of every single board member. They just need to know, clearly and succinctly, why something happened, why it won't happen again, and why the organization will be stronger going forward into the future."

Source: Kivi Miller, President, Nonprofit Marketing Guide.com, Lexington, NC. Phone (336) 499-5816. E-mail: Kivi@ecoscribe.com

49 Online Press Kits Simplify Reporters' Jobs, Increase Interest

If journalists find your website difficult to navigate, they may move on and you may miss out on media coverage.

Solve that problem with an online press kit.

Design your online press kit with the media in mind, says Amy Fisher, director of technology and agribusiness at public relations agency Padilla Speer Beardsley (Minneapolis, MN). "Your online press kit should not just be a collection of things you can find other places," she says. "It should contain things that are specific to the needs of the press."

Offer story ideas on your Web page, including names and contact information for people in your organization to be interviewed on the story topics, Fisher says. Add multi-media elements a reporter can use in the story (e.g., short quotes from board members, images and video clips).

Don't overdo your online press kit. Stick to a couple of key messages. Press releases, for instance, don't belong in an online press kit. They belong with the overall website. Provide a link to them from your online kit.

Finally, Fisher says, know that online press kits can be static to represent your overall organization, or event-specific, made available for a limited duration.

Source: Amy Fisher, Director of Technology and Agribusiness, Padilla Speer Beardsley, Minneapolis, MN. Phone (612) 455-1733. E-mail: afisher@psbpr.com

---

Online Press Kit Samples

Amy Fisher of the public relations agency Padilla Speer Beardsley (Minneapolis, MN) shares links for online press kits her firm has worked on recently:

❏ BASF Professional Pest Control (www.pestcontrolfacts.org/media/) — Basic information media need and links to topic experts on the Contact Us page.

❏ Mayo Clinic Health Manager (http://pub.psbpr.com/microsoft_mayo/CDMediaKit/mediakit.html) — Designed to launch Mayo Clinic Health Manager, this site includes a fact sheet and FAQ for information on the new service, plus a consumer tip sheet with an example of content media could repurpose.

❏ Automation Fair (http://pub.psbpr.com/Rockwell/AutomationFair2007MediaKit/mediakit_af.html) —This event-based press site includes a link for media to provide event feedback, event agendas and background materials on products media would see at the event.

---

50 Press Release Follow Up — Keep It Personal

You have e-mailed your press release to media outlets. Now what?

Joan Stewart, a media relations consultant and author of the online newsletter The Publicity Hound (Port Washington, WI), says, "A press release follow-up cannot be generic, it has to be customized and offer the media outlet something extra."

According to Stewart, too many organizations send out cookie-cutter press releases. Then they make a run-of-the-mill phone call to check and see if it arrived. That kind of follow-up call can actually hurt your chances of getting coverage in the long run, she says, because it makes the media representative feel as if you are wasting his/her time.

So how do you effectively follow up when you send a press release?

First, Stewart says, understand that a press release must be sent to a person and not a department. One to two days after you mail, fax or e-mail your press release, follow up with that specifically designated recipient. Whether you send an e-mail or make a phone call, what you should not do is ask, "Did you get my press release?" Instead try, "I sent you some information and I wanted to see if you needed anything else." That approach, the media expert says, makes reporters feel important and allows you a chance to bring up some extras that will pique their interest.

To further engage your media contact and increase the possibility of positive media coverage, Stewart says, offer suggestions for a photo or video to accompany the story and information on an idea for a side story or website link. For newspaper sources, for example, offer an easy-to-read Top 10 list of information related to the topic. For a TV or radio station, provide a website link to more information to further inform the audience and connect them to your cause.

The suggestions you pitch in a follow-up call should be customized for each media contact based on the media venue's core audience. For television and newspapers think people and visuals, Stewart says, "Give them a character."

Take the example of a press release for a fundraising dinner. Without proper follow-up it could get overlooked in a lot of newsrooms. However, when you call the reporter try something like, "Did I tell you about the 87-year-old we are honoring at the event? She's been volunteering for 37 years." The reporter will hear the potential for a story in that character versus just being asked to come and cover the event.

Source: Joan Stewart, Media Relations Consultant & Author, The Publicity Hound, Port Washington, WI. Phone (262)284-7451. E-mail: jstewart@publicityhound.com. Website: http://www.PublicityHound.com. Blog: http://www.PublicityHound.net

51 Create a Time Capsule To Celebrate Significant Events

Dedicating a new or renovated building is just one reason to consider creating a time capsule. Other reasons include celebrating a milestone anniversary, launching a major program or expanding your services to a greater geographic region.

A time capsule creates a built-in option for a special event 25 or 50 years down the line as the next generation unearths the treasure to see what memories are stored inside.

A time capsule event can also be an opportunity to generate media coverage while setting up opportunities for related media events.

To make the most of your time capsule dedication:

✓ **Stage a group photograph.** Gather volunteers, staff, board members and supporters to pose for a photo forming the numbers in the year you plan to open the capsule. Include some small children and babies who might be at the opening ceremony.

✓ **Hold a sneak preview of capsule items.** Invite media to film a display of photos, newspapers, clothing, technology or copies of speeches, and announce the time

and date of the ceremony to encourage attendance.

✓ **Give a demonstration on how to assemble a time capsule.** Special considerations like proper materials, items to avoid because they easily deteriorate or become unusable because technology changes may be an interesting way to draw newcomers to your organization.

✓ **Predict the future.** Gather supporters to write about their predictions for the year the time capsule will be opened. Host a coffee or lunch where the correct type of acid-free papers and inks are provided. If your time capsule is small, have a contest to determine which ones will be included, but save the others for a display both at your facility and online.

✓ **Host a children's activity.** A coloring contest, a joint mural scroll project that will fit into the capsule or donations of a favorite toy for children of the future can be fun ways to involve an audience who might still be here to see the capsule opened again.

52 Promote Your Cause With an Educational Series

Ever produced a commercial or online video for your organization? Consider taking it one step further and creating your own educational series.

Staff with the Community Reinvestment Association of North Carolina (Durham, NC) created a 13-episode Spanish-language telenova series, "Nuestro Barrio" (Our Neighborhood) during a several-month period from 2005 to 2006. Episodes included important financial literacy information woven into soap opera-style story lines.

Peter Skillern, executive director, says the idea for the telenova series came from Dilsey Davis, the association's director of media advocacy.

A pilot shot using funding from fair housing enforcement agencies was used to bring corporate sponsor Freddie Mac (McLean, VA) onboard. The project was also partially funded by the association, with a production cost of roughly $1 million for the series.

Davis served as the series creator, director and producer. They hired independent contractors, including gaffers, a writing team, sound technicians, videographer, set designer/builder, wardrobe and makeup artists, and actors. Filming took place at a local restaurant as well as a local warehouse where the team built a set. Local police officers served as actors. The pilot was shot during a three-week period, and all 13 episodes were completed in five months.

Before airing on television, the series was first previewed at a local premiere at the Carolina Theatre in Dur-

ham, NC and included a red carpet. Local dignitaries, representatives from Freddie Mac, the cast and crew and their families were invited.

The series aired on several television stations, reaching some 25 million households.

"Seventy percent of Latinos' TV consumption is from English-language television. The telenova series was a crossover product," says Skillern. "The WB stations in North and South Carolina ran the series, making it the first Spanish-language show on English-language television. In select markets the show has aired on Telemundo, Univision, WB, V-ME on cable, analog, digital and satellite TV."

To keep the important messages of the series going, more than 60,000 DVDs of the series have been given out to the public by Freddie Mac's numerous customers, such as Bank of America. Currently, the DVD is available for purchase through the association's website for $19.99.

For organizations considering creating an educational series, Skillern offers this advice: "Start small within your budget and distribute the video content on public access, websites, etc. Distribution is as important as content, so start with the end in mind of a consumer watching your show. In addition, ask for help from community-access television."

Source: Peter Skillern, Executive Director, Community Reinvestment Association of North Carolina, Durham, NC. Phone (919) 667-1557, ext. 22. E-mail: peter@cra-nc.org

53 Make a Point to Connect With Elected Officials

Reaching out to local politicians is easy and could prove to be vital for your organization. There are two main reasons to reach out to local government officials: for funding and for their attendance at events or press conferences.

The first step is to identify the local representatives in your area and contact them. If you don't have current contacts with the political offices in your area, begin by calling and introducing yourself. It might be helpful to send your organization's press kit along with a personal note. Request a meeting with a staff member to go over your organization's goals and find out if your representative is able to help you in some way.

If you are interested in partnering with a local representative and involving them in your press conferences and community events, make sure to develop a solid rapport so you can send invitations and press requests throughout the year.

If your local representatives are unable to assist your organization, ask them to recommend one of their colleagues who have an interest in the type of work that you do. It never hurts to ask.

The presence of an elected official at your next press conference or special event is an automatic media draw. By reaching out to local politicians and building relationships, you can increase your media coverage as well as enhance community relations.

54 Be Ready to Make Compelling Case With Stories on Hand

Nothing makes a stronger case for support than a first-person testimonial about how your organization changed someone's life. To ensure you feature such stories in every publication, speaking engagement and article:

- **Make sure everyone knows the importance of sharing these stories.** A program person may get a great story from a client or customer, and development staff may know a great reason why someone made a donation. Make sure volunteers, donors and the people you serve are also aware of your interest in compelling stories.

- **Make stories easy to capture.** Offer a Give-us-your-story-idea form in your office, at meetings and online or allow people to submit their information in any format

(e-mail, letter, phone call) to maximize the number of story ideas you receive.

- **Designate a point person.** This person should review and organize the stories and be in charge of archiving the older stories to keep things fresh.

- **Organize stories.** Depending on your mission, organize stories alphabetically by last name of the story subject, chronologically or by category (e.g., donor stories, client stories, program development, etc.).

- **Keep them handy.** You may choose to keep them in a binder in a central location and/or archive them on your computer network. The priority is making sure they are accessible to everyone who will need them and that everyone knows that location.

55 The Nose for News — Is Your Story Up to Snuff?

We all like to think our story is the best — the most emotional, the most powerful, the one people just can't live without experiencing.

But taking an impartial look at the story may reveal a lack of newsworthiness.

Use these criteria to help you create stories that deserve reporters' attention and prevent you from burning out your media contacts with lackluster submissions:

- ❑ **Why should people care?** Not every story is worthy of media attention. A story that simply tells what your organization does, day in and day out, is not news. It is imperative that you have a reason you can pitch to reporters why people are going to be compelled to read this story — why their newspaper or broadcast can't do without the story you're offering. In the competitive

marketplace it has to be that good. To find out, run your story past a few people and ask them if it would hold their interest. Just make sure those people aren't as close to the story as you are.

- ❑ **Which markets?** Television stations need great visuals and both TV and radio stations need ear-catching sound bites. Can't deliver? Pitch your story to print media instead.

- ❑ **What does your story do for them?** Maybe your local organization has a connection to a current national trend or phenomenon. The link that you can provide to their readers or viewers can be invaluable.

- ❑ **Is it exclusive?** If your topic is of real interest to people, offering it as an exclusive might help get it picked up. That hot topic could increase sales or viewers — in some cases, even ad revenue — for the media outlet that gets it.

56 Great Lead Guides Readers to the Real Treat

"Writing great leads is like leaving a trail of bread crumbs throughout your article," says blogger and writer Laurie Pawlik-Kienlen (Vancouver, BC). "Your reader won't rest until he's eaten every last crumb."

Pawlik-Kienlen shares tactics to make your lead irresistible:

✓ **Be dramatic.** Including a dramatic fact makes introductions more interesting. Do you know that you are only reaching a small fraction of the number of people who need your service? Lead with the number and a call to action.

✓ **Be provocative.** "Provocative doesn't necessarily have to be sensual," says Pawlik-Kienlen. "Anything challenging, stimulating or even confrontational is provocative.

Writing great leads can involve catching your readers off-guard with a bit of controversy."

✓ **Be startling.** Grab readers' attention by leading with an eye-popping fact related to your mission or those you serve (e.g., the number of children who go to bed hungry every day).

Perhaps the most important point to remember is to not be timid. "Grab your reader by the throat," Pawlik-Kienlen says. Do so, and they will keep reading.

Source: Laurie Pawlik-Kienlen, Full-time Blogger and Freelance Writer, Creator of Quips and Tips for Successful Writers, Bowen Island, Vancouver, British Columbia, Canada. Phone (604) 947-0686. Website: http://theadventurouswriter.com

57 Get Fit Challenge Gives Makeover to Public's Perception

If your organization appears one-dimensional in your community, look for ways to expand your image and grow your support base.

Chris Grev, marketing and communications, United Way of Mower County, Inc. (Austin, MN), says her organization wanted to be known for something other than coming around once a year asking for money.

"We were also looking to get involved in our community, county wide on something not fundraising related," Grev says. "The popularity of the 'Biggest Loser' (an NBC television show about weight loss), along with the community's concerns about obesity led us to create The Get Fit Mower County Healthy Living Challenge."

The first year, the challenge was strictly a weight loss team competition, with participants receiving T-shirts and goodie bags filled with coupons, recipe booklets and water bottles. Grev says they were completely surprised when 924 individuals signed up.

The challenge has since grown to include a family challenge; a school component in which physical education classes throughout the county receive pedometers and walking maps for each school; education in the high schools about wise food choices; and a fitness challenge for individuals who don't want to lose weight, but want to become more active or maintain their level of activity.

While the challenge is a lot of work, Grev says, it's worth it.

"We now have visibility in many areas of the county we weren't penetrating before," Grev says, "and have seen an increase in overall fundraising dollars. We also have the privilege of bringing the community together around a very important issue and seeing real change take place where we live. We have seen many positive changes in our community and in others as a result of the program. That's the whole point behind the program."

Source: Chris Grev, Marketing and Communications, United Way of Mower County, Inc., Austin, MN. Phone (507) 437-2313. E-mail: unitedcg@smig.net

Four Tips for Healthy Collaboration

Chris Grev, marketing and communications, United Way of Mower County, Inc. (Austin, MN), says The Get Fit/Be Fit Challenge (detailed at left) has been a great way to collaborate with other businesses in the community, including other nonprofit organizations. "We're able to pool our resources, delegate responsibilities and maximize what we have to offer in the community to get the biggest bang for our buck," she says.

Grev shares tips to help collaborations run smoothly:

1. **Keep everyone in the loop.** Grev says electronic media is a great way to communicate quickly and easily and distribute information to partners and participants in an efficient and inexpensive manner.

2. **Adopt a "more the merrier" attitude.** This brings in more people to identify and deal with event issues while offsetting expenses and workload.

3. **Determine up front who will have final say if conflicts arise.** Grev says they have not encountered any difficult decisions or choices. However, as the lead agency on the program, United Way would have final say in decisions.

4. **Map out responsibilities in advance.** "This allows each of us to work on our part of the program and do it well," says Grev. "When there are too many tasks on one plate, something gets missed."

58   Notable Figures Tie the Past to the Present

Finding a natural fit between your organization and a notable historical figure — whether that be a founder of your organization or someone instrumental in influencing your mission — can allow you to draw attention and historically mark special events within your organization.

Calvin College (Grand Rapids, MI) was named for theologian John Calvin, who was born in 1509. The college is celebrating the 500th anniversary of its namesake's birth with events throughout the year, from conferences to on-campus events to formal and less-formal ceremonies.

Dedicating an entire year to celebrate Calvin's birth benefits the college in many ways, says Phil de Haan, director of communications and marketing.

Here, de Haan answers questions about the year-long celebration:

How does connecting to a notable figure of the past amplify an event?

"History is important, but history is especially important at a place such as Calvin College, which was established in Grand Rapids in 1876, and which takes its name from a famous theologian who was born in the 1500s. Taking the time to celebrate today what is lasting and worthwhile about events and people from long ago is a way for a place like Calvin to understand its past and also look ahead to the future. Former Calvin President William Spoelhof had an expression he liked to use about Calvin's responsibilities to past, present and future. He said we needed to be 'grateful to our ancestors, faithful to our heirs.' Connecting an event to a figure from the past is a good way to do that — to recognize those leaders who came before us as we educate and empower the next generation."

By celebrating John Calvin's birthday, did you generate excitement within the college's community?

"In the summer there are fewer opportunities on a college campus for people to come together. Although we offer some summer school classes at Calvin, the majority of our students are not here during the summer months. So having something like a celebration of John Calvin's birthday allows people to get together, to enjoy some cake and punch and to catch up a little. This year we added a short video to the celebration which put a little different twist on things and gave people another reason to laugh and have some fun."

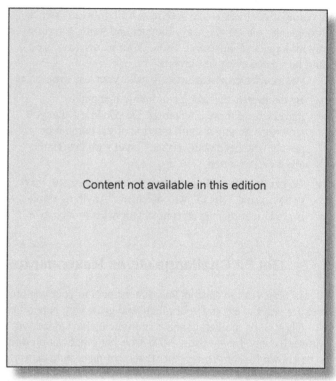

Content not available in this edition

By making this connection to the college, did it draw more media attention?

"We gained media attention as a result of the event, including a nice NPR interview that the director of our center for Calvin studies did, but it really was not planned or intended solely as a media event. Media coverage was a side benefit. In addition we gave the event some of our own coverage on our Calvin website (www.calvin.edu), including posting the video on (the online video sharing site) Vimeo (www.vimeo.com), creating a photo album and more. We also posted it to our Calvin Facebook page (www.facebook.com/CalvinCollege) and our Calvin Twitter feed (www.twitter.com/calvincollege)."

What's your best tip to another organization who wants to connect a notable figure to a current event to draw more attendees or attention?

"Look for places to connect that are authentic and that make sense for your organization."

Source: Phil de Haan, Director of Communications and Marketing, Calvin College, Grand Rapids, MI. Phone (616) 526-6142. E-mail: dehp@calvin.edu

59   Highlight Press Releases With a Media Blog

Create a media relations blog to spotlight press releases and include interactive features.

In September 2007, the media relations team at Lourdes College (Sylvania, OH) launched a media relations blog specifically to post press releases. Written by staff, students and alumni, the blog's goal is to communicate the most current Lourdes news to the public, says Heather Hoffman, media coordinator and chief author of the blog.

"Media has become so interactive, that I just don't think the typical press release, all text and no action, packs the same pizzazz that an interactive tool like a blog has," says Hoffman. While they still post press releases in an online newsroom, "I enjoy using the blog to post press releases because it allows others to give feedback and comment on stories. It also offers features that typical attachments do not," such as the ability to embed videos, slideshows and photos.

The college's Web content administrator and the director of college relations, in conjunction with Thread Information Design (Maumee, OH), created the blog center that includes the media relations blog and others related to the college.

Response from staff, students, alumni and the community has been positive, says Hoffman, noting that the local media has noticed the releases listed on the blog as well.

For nonprofits considering a media blog, Hoffman offers this advice: "Be as interactive as possible. Post videos, photos and allow for dialogue. This will give your reporting an added touch that a typical press release falls short of. Don't be afraid to make your media a dynamic experience!"

Source: Heather Hoffman, Media Coordinator, Lourdes College, Sylvania, OH. Phone (419) 824-3952.

60   Book Signings Create Interest, Generate Publicity

Hosting a book signing is a powerful way to generate publicity for your organization, especially if the author is a staff member or has another connection with your cause.

"We organize book signings regularly for Whitworth University (Spokane, WA) faculty and administrators who publish books," says Greg Orwig, director of communications. "We also have book signings for many lecturers and authors who come to campus for lectures or readings."

Each year they host at least two signings on campus and one off campus at a local bookstore.

"We usually line these up through local bookstores that offer book readings and signings as part of their community outreach," says Orwig. "We have one large independent store and one branch of a national chain that are regular hosts of Whitworth. This is one of those things that are a win-win for all concerned, the bookstore, the author and the university."

Orwig says a major benefit of hosting a book signing is its relatively low cost. "We don't incur any costs for readings hosted by local bookstores and very little cost for readings we host on campus, unless we pay an honorarium for bringing the author to campus for the lecture/reading."

English department staff organize two readings a year, choosing authors whose works they feel would appeal to a broad audience. "The university often brings other guest speakers to campus who have recently published books. Sometimes these authors have books that are used in or are assigned for classes," says Orwig. "Regardless, our campus bookstore orders a supply of books to have on hand for sale and signing purposes."

Attendance varies depending on factors such as book topic and author popularity, he says: "When we had former U.S. Poet Laureate Billy Collins and Anne Lamott on campus, we packed our largest venue on campus, which holds just over 1,200. For lesser-known authors, we sometimes draw in dozens. Off-campus signings have ranged from 10 to about 50. All kinds of variables can affect those numbers, but the most important one, I think, is the accessibility/perceived relevance of the book title and subject."

For on-site book signings, Orwig recommends inviting the author to do a lecture or reading from the book along with the signing. Make sure you have an appropriate venue available to set up a table and chair in a space that can readily accommodate a line up, as well as an ample supply of books available and a means to sell them, including collecting the sales tax if applicable. "We arrange that through our campus bookstore," he says. "If that's not an option, it may be possible to coordinate it through a local bookstore."

When hosting a book signing, Orwig recommends taking pictures and getting quotes from the authors to use in internal and external communications materials. University staff often turn lectures and readings into podcasts on their website. Orwig cautions that it is necessary to obtain a signed release from the author in order to do this.

If hosting an on-site signing is not an option, he advises contacting local bookstores to see what policies are on book signings. Since the university has a long-term relationship with their local bookstores, setting up each signing is an easy task. However, Orwig recommends checking in with all of your local bookstores on a regular basis to see if their policies regarding signings have changed.

Source: Greg Orwig, Director of Communications, Whitworth University, Spokane, WA. Phone (509) 777-4580.

61 Community Profiles Add Personal Insight

Consider adding personal and professional profiles to your organization's website to bring a broader understanding to the work your organization does.

Community profiles are an element added in the recent redesign of the website for Seattle Children's (Seattle, WA). The home page of www.seattlechildrens.org features the link, "Celebrating Members of Our Community," that takes visitors to online profiles of a scientist, family member and supporter of the hospital.

Chris Tobey, creative services director at Seattle Children's, corporate communications, says they generally create online profiles on one of three audiences: people who do the work of Seattle Children's (researchers, clinicians, staff); those served by the hospital (patients and families, and those who might benefit from the advocacy and safety efforts); or those who support the organization (donors, guild members, volunteers).

"Through the work we do on a variety of projects, the marketing and communications and foundation teams at Seattle Children's always hear compelling stories about the people in our communities," says Tobey. "In addition, folks throughout our organization send recommendations and ideas. Currently, decisions about whom to profile are made in marketing and communications, and only with permission of those being profiled.

"Pediatric healthcare and medical research are about people and the hope for a healthy life and better future," says Tobey. "These profiles help illustrate, in a personal way, the purpose of our organization's work, the impact this work has on those we serve, and the key role members of our community play in supporting our work."

Source: Chris Tobey, Creative Services Director, Seattle Children's, Seattle, WA. Phone (206) 987-5268.
E-mail: chris.tobey@seattlechildrens.org.
Website: www.seattlechildrens.org

62 Thorough Preparation Can Help With Walk Through Fire

Toyota is feeling the pressure. So is Tiger Woods. Their reputations are under fire, and only time will tell whether they will survive.

To think that your organization is immune to similar scrutiny is foolhardy.

According to Jan Smith, principal, Castle Rock Ranch Group, LLC (Loudonville, NY), and reputation management consultant, lots of good organizations get caught when something bad happens because they weren't prepared. "Preparation starts by thinking about the personality of your brand," Smith says. "Toyota still makes cars. How people feel about them is what changed."

Smith says the following tips will help prepare you for any eventuality:

✓ **Plan ahead.** Take time as a staff to ask these questions: Who are we? What do we stand for? What are the messages we want to get across? Then get it on paper, even if it's only one page. Smith says working genuinely to convey who you are before a crisis will go a long way to help you in a crisis. "These messages are who you are, not the crisis. If people already know you as an organization before a crisis, and know that you do the right thing, they know you'll do the right thing in the face of a crisis."

✓ **Know your advocates.** Knowing which third parties will speak on your behalf has more value than any ad campaign or media blitz. "Think about where it is most important for your organization to have connections so people know you, understand you and believe in you," says Smith.

✓ **Play what if.** Brainstorm the four or five most likely, horrible scenarios your organization could face. Consider what questions might be asked and write your responses. Decide on a chain of contact and make sure the press knows it.

✓ **Consider your resources.** Are there some situations that may require help from outside PR resources? If you think you would need additional help at some point, figure out whom that would be now and put them on alert.

✓ **Recognize your role.** Nonprofits are a vital part of the local community and no one wants to see that go bad, Smith says. Remember this when conveying your message.

Smith says the best way to be prepared is to behave naturally with proper background and training. "It's about mixing good judgment with concern. People want to know what you know and what's going to happen next. They also want to know you are concerned and that you are genuine. If you're prepared, there's a 100 percent chance you'll do well."

Source: Jan Smith, Principal, Castle Rock Ranch Group, LLC, Loudonville, NY. Phone (518) 301-3067.
E-mail: jan@castlerockranch.com

63 Use Construction Period to Point to Progress

If facility construction or renovation is taking place at your nonprofit and you're not inviting the media, donors and others to witness the changes taking place, you're missing a great opportunity.

For most nonprofits, a period of major construction/renovation is an infrequent occurrence. And when it does take place — even if it is somewhat messy — most people will perceive the changes being made as progress. The noise, the construction workers, the chaos surrounding the project are all perceived as steps toward an enhanced environment.

To get the most from your organization's construction project:

1. Invite small groups of individuals to view the project at various points during the construction phase. Think about whether it's to your advantage to mix members of the media with donors or community leaders or target each group separately. Both have their advantages.

2. Pay attention to detail after guests arrive. Depending on the size and scope of your construction project, you may wish to make golf carts available for tours. Pay particular attention to safety factors. You may decide to distribute hard hats, for instance.

3. Have persons present who can point out changes taking place and how those changes will impact those served by your organization.

4. Conclude the tour with refreshments and brief remarks by your CEO or board chair.

Make it a standard practice to set follow-up appointments with attendees to answer questions or pursue feature possibilities.

64 Launch a Marketing Campaign That Creates Mystery

Most people enjoy a little mystery in their lives. The marketing team at The Phoenix Zoo (Phoenix, AZ) recently capitalized on that to create a successful campaign for the debut of their newest exhibit — Land of the Dragons.

"We created an air of intrigue around the new exhibit, not revealing what was to live there," says Trish Bump, director of marketing and corporate relations. "Our marketing only hinted at a large reptile from the jungle, with menacing images of sharp teeth and claws."

> *"We created an air of intrigue around the new exhibit.... Our marketing only hinted at a large reptile from the jungle, with menacing images of sharp teeth and claws."*

First came the billboards and bus wraps with a warning: "It's Coming." Artwork featured the eye of a strange creature staring at passersby. Shortly after came the addition of a sharp claw and the tag line, "claws, teeth, and all." Radio stations played ads featuring jungle sound effects and an ominous voice-over, "It's coming."

The Phoenix Zoo is one of America's most successful, privately owned, nonprofit zoological parks, serving more than 1.5 million guests annually. Its Land of the Dragons exhibit debuted in November 2009 and features two Komodo dragons indigenous to the islands of Indonesia.

"As the zoo's first new exhibit in several years, it's a compelling reason for people to visit," says Bump. "So we needed to create a marketing campaign that was just as compelling."

The teaser campaign eventually included a contest that challenged locals to guess the mystery animal. More than 1,000 peopled entered the contest at the zoo's dedicated website for the exhibit, www.landofthedragons.org.

Local corporate partners were also recruited to get in on the fun. Coca-Cola promoted the exhibit with a discounted zoo admission offer on its trucks and vending machines. A local grocery store chain intrigued shoppers with teaser materials at the entrance and signs placed throughout the store, while employees wore T-shirts with the image of the dragon and Land of the Dragon exhibit.

Throughout the campaign, Bump's team also used social media to tease followers and fans about the attraction. Via Twitter (www.twitter.com), more than 3,500 followers were given hints and plugs on what was coming. On Facebook (www.facebook.com), the campaign generated buzz with chances to win tickets to the zoo and its new exhibit.

Source: Trish Bump, Director of Marketing & Corporate Relations, Phoenix Zoo, Phoenix, AZ. Phone (480) 603-6088. E-mail: tbump@thephxzoo.com. Website: www.phoenixzoo.org

65 Engage Supporters, Community With Name Our Mascot Contest

Does your organization have a mascot or are you thinking of adding one? Host a contest to name the mascot to familiarize your supporters, community and local news media with the project while providing some great naming ideas.

Staff with Butler University (Indianapolis, IN) created a mascot-naming contest after people were confused about what to call the mascot, known simply as the Butler Bulldog, following a costume theft, says Lindsay Martin, manager, sports marketing & promotions.

"When our original costumes were stolen in August '08, there was some confusion among the news media and general public over what to call the bulldog costumes. Many were calling it Blue, which is actually the name of our live English bulldog mascot," says Martin. "That led to calls from fans thinking that the actual dog had been stolen. So we decided that by giving the costume a name of its own, we'd clear up any future confusion."

After two weeks of planning, they had the contest up and running. They publicized it first internally to faculty, staff and students via e-mail, then promoted it at basketball games, on the university's website, on the mascot's Facebook page and on the live mascot's blog at www.butlerblue2.blogspot.com. They also publicized the contest to regional media outlets that covered the theft of the original costumes.

Community members submitted nearly 300 unique name suggestions online or in person at home basketball games. A nine-person committee (administrators from student affairs, university relations and athletics) narrowed this list down to a handful of entries. Fans then voted online and at basketball games for their favorite.

Officials announced the winning name, Hink, at a Jan. 22, 2009, men's basketball game, presenting the mascot with a team jersey emblazoned with the name.

The prize package for the four winners, all of whom submitted the name Hink, included four courtside seats to the game and a VIP experience with parking, programs and concessions.

"We wanted a prize that was an experience, as opposed to just something they would put on a shelf," says Martin.

For organizations planning on creating a mascot naming contest, Martin recommends allowing the public to vote

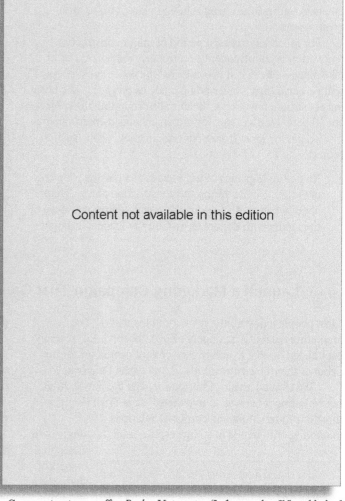

Content not available in this edition

Communications staff at Butler University (Indianapolis, IN) published results of a Name Our Mascot campaign with this website article.

online as it will allow supporters far and wide to participate. In addition, she recommends narrowing down submissions to a handful of finalists that the public can choose from instead of letting them choose from a larger pool of random entries.

Source: Lindsay Martin, Manager, Sports Marketing & Promotions, Butler University, Hinkle Fieldhouse, Indianapolis, IN. Phone (317) 940-9468. E-mail: lmartin@butler.edu

66 Find Attention-grabbing Ideas To Celebrate Milestones

Milestone anniversaries present opportunities to reach out to new audiences throughout the celebration year. Like birthdays, anniversaries — especially those marking significant years such as 25, 50 or 100 — are the perfect time to spread good will and good news.

Here are just a few ideas to do so:

✓ **Form a speakers' bureau.** Your organization likely has several people prepared to give presentations about its past, present and future to service clubs, social and business groups, chambers of commerce and schools. Make the most effective speakers available for media interviews as well.

✓ **Launch community outreach programs.** This is an ideal time to begin a service that expands your scope. Venture into job training, preventative health or other areas that coincide with your mission while filling a need.

✓ **Host birthday events all year.** Invite the community to celebrate with you several times during the year through spring marathon walks or runs, a summer concert series and a Founder's Day party with cake and all the trimmings. Make events family friendly to boost attendance.

✓ **Publish an advertising supplement.** Choose a local news or business publication to produce a full-color special edition featuring stories and photos about your history; interviews from longtime employees, board members or volunteers; current goals and activities, and leadership strategies to lead you forward. Invite vendors and others to buy ads, and print extra copies to distribute after the original run.

✓ **Create an anniversary logo.** Put the logo on all printed materials, billboards and advertising, as well as items available for purchase, like polo shirts, caps, plates, jewelry or bags. Sell them in your gift shop, online or give to new donors or volunteers.

✓ **Celebrate construction.** The timing may be right to announce a construction or landscaping project. Donors may purchase engraved bricks for a special wall or walkway, trees or statues in a peaceful courtyard, or artwork in a newly renovated area of your building.

67 Consider These Techniques for Writing Vibrant Client Features

Every organization has clients, patients, volunteers or students who have success stories related to the organization's mission. Deciding how to best tell those stories is the first step in sharing them with the public.

Consider these angles to determine the most effective means by which to share stories about persons benefiting from your mission:

❏ **Write an As-told-to article.** The subject can share his or her thoughts and experiences candidly in his/her own words, but leave the actual writing in the hands of a professional who can identify the most relevant aspects to include in the story.

❏ **Mix journal excerpts with editorial.** Some people enjoy keeping journals while they are going through medical challenges, rehabilitation, or as a way of handling life-changing events like loss of a family member or career change. When your organization has helped them through those times, an article that includes their thoughts at the time adds more dimension.

❏ **Interview involved staff.** While keeping your client or patient as the focus of your article, include comments from those who assisted him/her on the road to success. Members of the medical team who formulated the treatment plan, counselors who helped identify his/her true vocation or mentors who offered guidance can contribute to the overall story.

❏ **Take a photojournalism approach.** Pictures can tell a client's story in a highly personal way, showing struggle, determination, contemplation, teamwork, self-discovery and the joy of accomplishment. Once you have identified a potential success story, be there for important steps in his or her journey through your programs.

❏ **Create a video diary and article.** Reality television shows often give subjects video cameras so they can record their concerns when film crews are off duty. Footage of your subjects sharing their thoughts the day before an important job interview or medical procedure, or their reactions the day after, can be combined with editorial for a fascinating online article.

Make Use of Anniversary Postcards

Is your organization about to celebrate a milestone anniversary? How about searching through old photographs and turning a few into attractive postcards that include brief descriptions of them on the back side? Here are ideas for putting the postcards to good use:

• Offer a set of postcards as a premium to those who make contributions at a certain level.

• Use postcards to announce special anniversary events throughout the year.

• Invite your employees to use them throughout the year for correspondence — personal notes to the media, donors, clients (students, patients, members) and others.

• Sell sets of the postcards in your bookstore or gift shop.

 Highlight Notable Media Coverage

When your organization receives stellar coverage in the print news media, make the most of this recognition by posting the article in your office. Doing so will catch the attention of your co-workers and other visitors while serving as a source of motivation.

Tanya L. Grady, communications coordinator, Provincetown Center for Coastal Studies (Provincetown, MA), displays a March 2009 story from The Boston Globe in her office.

"I chose to post this piece because the reporter got the story right and the piece was prominently displayed in the paper," says Grady. "The piece specifically brings to light the many challenges a particular species faces and its struggle to recover from the brink of extinction, and it also explains my organization's research and our work to aid this population in its recovery.

"Posting articles reminds me of my accomplishments and motivates me, but I think that it also demonstrates my ability as a coordinator to maximize exposure and advance the goals of my organization," Grady says. "I hope posting articles sends a message of competence and provides tangible evidence of my contribution to others."

Additionally, she says, showcasing print media coverage in this way "reminds you when it's time to push forward and secure fresh coverage or strategize for a new media campaign or blitz."

Source: Tanya L. Grady, Communications Coordinator, Provincetown Center for Coastal Studies, Provincetown, MA. Phone (508) 247-7665. E-mail: tgrady@coastalstudies.org

 Day in the District Shows Local Leaders a Day in the Life

If you're looking for a way to show that donor dollars are being used in a quality and efficient manner, consider offering opportunities for donors to shadow some of your workers.

That's what the staff at the Harris County Hospital District (HCHD) Foundation (Houston, TX) have done with their Day in the District program.

The program has been a great success, says Katie Mears, special events manager.

"At first it was hard convincing people to spend an entire day with us," Mears says, "but at the end of the day everyone is convinced it was totally worth their time."

So what is involved in promoting and pulling off a day-in-the-life event that draws both praise from participants and positive media coverage? Careful planning and matching participants with their experiences.

Day in the District provides an inside look at the job local nurses and physicians do each day to serve uninsured and underinsured patients. Participants are individually paired with doctors and nurses for four rotations throughout the day, in which they have hands-on experiences in services such as surgery, physical therapy, psychiatry, the emergency

center, social work, pathology and other specialty clinics.

The day concludes with a roundtable dinner and discussion with the hospital district CEO, COO and other administrators.

Participants include community leaders, local journalists,

"At first it was hard convincing people to spend an entire day with us, but at the end of the day everyone is convinced it was totally worth their time."

donors and prospective donors. Past participants also make recommendations. Invitations from the CEO are sent out a few months in advance.

Mears says the idea was conceived after they realized there was a greater need for community understanding of the public health care system in their county. Day in the District has not only provided that, but has also helped develop relationships with participants that have evolved into roles as board members, volunteers and advocates for HCHD. Not bad for a day's work!

Source: Katie Mears, Special Events Manager, HCHD Foundation, Houston, TX. Phone (713) 556-6409. E-mail: Mary_Mears@hchd.tmc.edu

71 Increase Media Exposure With a Faculty Expert Program

At one level, the faculty expert program at Villanova University (Villanova, PA) is a simple thing: a website putting media representatives in touch with faculty members available for interview. But the program accomplishes far more than that, says Jonathan Gust, director of media relations.

The program "assists the media, but it also serves as a mechanism to increase institutional visibility and highlight the world-class strength of our faculty and staff," he says. "It's a way to regularly put our name in front of the public."

The media relations department, which launched the program shortly after its inception in 2007, schedules media interviews and provides background and guidance on which faculty experts could best speak on particular topics. It also works with key department heads to recruit faculty to the program. Over 150 professors currently participate, but Gust expects that number to double as the program continues to develop.

Each participating expert is listed by name, title, area of expertise and biographical overview on the program's website. Information on education, professional experience, publications and research is also provided.

All aspects of the site are tailored to the needs of media contacts, Gust says. "The goal is to create a one-stop media shop — the kind of place professionals like and would want to return to."

Because the faculty profiles need to be updated regularly, the program demands significant resources. But Gust says the effort is well worth the trouble. "The media is constantly looking for spokespeople to speak on areas of breaking news, and the faculty expert program positions us as a reliable and valuable resource."

The program currently accommodates 20 to 25 requests a week.

Source: Jonathan Gust, Director of Media Relations, Villanova University, Villanova. PA. Phone (610) 519-6508. E-mail: jonathan.gust@villanova.edu. Website: www.villanova.edu/communication/media

72 Make Sure Employee-of-the-month Program Doesn't Backfire

Employee-of-the-month programs set out to reward, recognize and show appreciation for standout workers. While they're designed to inspire your staff, Gregory P. Smith, business strategist with Chart Your Course International Inc. (Conyers, GA), says, "Most of the employee-of-the-month programs I have seen rarely work as intended."

The problem? Fairness.

Traditional programs rely on supervisors to nominate one of their employees for recognition each month. Smith points out that some people may deserve recognition, but work for managers who do not take the time to nominate anyone.

In a small work environment, he says, the typical monthly award may actually defeat teamwork. Winners can feel uncomfortable being selected and those who never get the award can feel ignored and unappreciated.

"Small firms can fall into the trap of giving the award to only a few top performers or be forced to rotate the award from person to person, whether they deserve it or not, just to meet the monthly requirement," says Smith.

So how do you make your program work for you, not against you?

According to Smith, the programs that work the best are those that are run by employees, with winners nominated by peers. Top performers aren't the only ones who should be recognized, he adds; some of the most meaningful programs focus on values, outstanding service and day-to-day encounters.

Two examples of employee-run recognition programs can be found at the University of Michigan (UM), Ann Arbor, MI and the University of Missouri – St. Louis (UMSL), St. Louis, MO.

For UM's U Matter award, staff members submit online nominations for actions coworkers have taken to make people feel like they matter. Each of the 10 winners receives a U Matter pin.

Because of the eclectic nature of the nominations, the program allows supervisors to be more aware of great things their employees are doing that otherwise may go unnoticed, says Rose Bernal, human resources administrative assistant, adding, "Sometimes the winners don't even realize that they've had such an impact on their peers."

At UMSL a winner is selected by a broadly representative committee that bases its decision on themes that vary from month to month. For example, May's award honors innovation and creativity, while June's will go to the employee who is a superb communicator. UMSL's awards can range from a pin or plaque to a gift certificate to the winner's favorite restaurant.

Smith says awards don't have to cost a lot to make an impact; his advice is to keep it simple and fun. For example, he says, "One staff takes the winner out for breakfast each month and provides them with a reserved parking space near their office's front door."

Sources: Rose Bernal, Human Resources Administrative Assistant, University of Michigan, Ann Arbor, MI. Phone (734) 936-3549. Website: www.hr.umich.edu/umatter/index.html
Sylvia Poe, Human Resources Assistant Director, University of Missouri – St. Louis, St. Louis, MO. Phone (314) 516-5258. Website: www.umsl.edu/services/hrs/current/eom_info.html
Gregory P. Smith, Business Strategist & Lead Navigator, Chart Your Course International Inc., Conyers, GA. Phone (770) 860-9464. Website: http://ChartCourse.com

73 Tweets Keep Your Stories on the Beat

How are you using social media to generate positive publicity for your cause?

Michael Schwartzberg, media relations manager, Greater Baltimore Medical Center (Baltimore, MD) and former journalist, says Twitter may just be the next big thing for distributing press releases and media advisories.

Start by signing up at www.twitter.com to receive Tweets (brief messages) from local reporters to stay abreast of new members of the local media landscape, learn who has left and what beats have changed.

Schwartzberg says he also sends Tweets with a URL link to press releases on his organization's website.

Source: Michael Schwartzberg, Media Relations Manager, Greater Baltimore Medical Center, Baltimore, MD. Phone (443) 849-2126. E-mail: mschwartzberg@gbmc.org

> **Twitter 101**
>
> Twitter is an instant messenger service that allows users to send brief messages to subscribed recipients using the Internet, mobile texting or similar venues. Twitter messages, called Tweets, are limited to 140 characters, allowing for quick updates, reminders, group thank yous or calls to action. Learn more at www.twitter.com.

74 Tout Your Organization's Multiple Achievements

People like giving to winning causes. Show how important headway is being made in fulfilling your mission and meeting strategic goals, and your potential customers, donors, volunteers and others will want to be associated with your winning organization.

Here are ideas to help you pinpoint where you might be leading the pack:

- How your services compare to regional/national averages.
- The achievements of those served by you — students, youth, members, etc.
- Accomplishments of individual and/or collective employees.
- Honors, awards and citations directed to your organization.

- Financial feats — low administrative costs, balanced budgets, endowment growth.
- Comparisons to highly respected organizations that reflect positively.
- Relationship to certain regional/national trends that position you favorably.
- Longevity issues — years of continued service, employee tenure, etc.
- Statistics that distinguish your organization from the crowd — "One of every five high school superintendents throughout the state is a graduate of our school."
- Good deeds — community service projects, employee involvement in civic affairs.

75 Five Ways to Showcase Your Organization's Stories

The larger your nonprofit's scope, the greater the potential for great stories about the people you touch. To identify subjects and people to generate the coverage your organization deserves:

❏ **Be a historian.** Familiarity with your organization's past helps you discover links to its future. It may have a long history of programs supporting women's issues, child advocacy, helping laid-off workers find new careers or other timely topics. Pave the way for an article about your organization's pioneering spirit and continuity of mission.

❏ **Get into the trenches.** Shadow your staff or volunteers for a few days. See what they do for people your organization serves, and get to know some of those who benefited, like the young single mother who found a good job through one of your programs or the great-grandmother who is enjoying needlepoint again because of new eyeglasses you provided.

❏ **Ask supporters for ideas.** Your newsletter or website is a great vehicle for asking supporters to tell you about a

good story with a happy result because of your services. If your readers know you want such ideas, most won't hesitate to share them. Making these a regular feature will encourage even more leads that you can parlay into human-interest stories.

❏ **Stay abreast of local and national news.** Perhaps your community has a wave of newly minted American citizens or has recovered from a plant closing and is back to full employment. Did your organization assist in those efforts to earn citizenship or find jobs? Look for some of the best examples illustrating your progressive partnerships for news articles.

❏ **Have a good hook.** Your organization delivers on its mission every day, so avoid pitching the routine for media coverage. Look to spotlight how that mission is changing lives. For example, when the child of the Sudanese family you have been helping earns a full academic scholarship to the university, the inspiring development has broad news appeal.

You Can't Beat Word-of-mouth Marketing

Want the public to become more aware of your organization's valuable services and programs? Then get those you serve and loyal supporters to talk it up.

Nothing beats satisfied customers when it comes to attracting more customers, donors and others. Serve as a catalyst helping others to spread the word by:

✓ Offering periodic training sessions that serve to educate loyal supporters on ways they can help.

✓ Meeting with interested groups and individuals, asking them to serve as ambassadors on behalf of your nonprofit.

✓ Publishing and distributing a quarterly handout for insiders that lists ways they can augment your marketing efforts. Include examples of how others have promoted your organization in recent months.

Media Campaign Boosts Gifts, Awareness, Volunteer Numbers

Increasing awareness of your organization can lead to significant payoffs, just as it did for Open Hand (Atlanta, GA), a volunteer-driven nonprofit that provides meals and nutrition education to help people better manage chronic disease.

Open Hand's recent multipurpose media campaign produced big results in terms of awareness, donors, donations and volunteers, says John Penninger, director of marketing.

"On the cusp of Open Hand's 20th anniversary, the organization developed a new brand identity which better reflects our new vision and mission and our focus on prevention-based nutrition," says Penninger. "The campaign was designed to launch this new brand, raise awareness of the vital work we do in the community and keep up with the increased demand for volunteers."

Boost in New Volunteers is Campaign's Most Significant Trend

Within six months of the campaign, Penninger says, they experienced a 30 percent increase in donors, 28 percent increase in individual giving and 58 percent increase in volunteers.

"Since our charge was not only to make new audiences aware of Open Hand and the work we do, but to ensure that our existing volunteers and donors were aware of our expanded mission and refreshed brand, we knew going in that overall awareness would be difficult to quantify," Penninger says. "What's more, we simply did not have the funds to conduct any meaningful post-campaign research to measure it.

"Over time, we did identify some significant trends that seemed to indicate that the campaign was a verifiable success. The most obvious was the dramatic increase in new volunteers, especially the number of volunteers from outside the metro Atlanta area. In addition, corporate volunteer groups and overall donor activity showed significant increases."

Majority of Budget Goes Toward Radio Spots

The concentrated three-month media schedule consisted of two 60-second radio ads, three 14 X 48-foot outdoor ads and two limited print ads that ran as public service announcements. Approximately 75 percent of the $150,000 campaign budget,

Content not available in this edition

Billboards such as this helped build awareness, bring in donors and attract volunteers for Open Hand (Atlanta, GA).

funded primarily by a group of donors, went toward radio ads, with the remainder going for billboards.

"Metropolitan Atlanta is a large, commuter-oriented city, a scenario in which radio and outdoor perfectly complement each other," Penninger says. "An effective mix of radio stations and a highly targeted outdoor presence reinforced Open Hand's new brand positioning and helped make the organization top-of-mind. In addition, outdoor allowed us to launch our new brand with high visual impact, while radio provided an opportunity for our volunteers to relate their own personal experiences with Open Hand."

Professional Media Buyer Uses Expertise to Reach Target Audience on a Budget

To make a big impact on a limited budget, Open Hand officials used a media strategist to negotiate with radio stations for an affordable plan that reached the diverse audiences they sought to reach with the campaign. This is a strategy Penninger recommends.

"Working with an experienced media buyer as you plan your campaign can prove to be invaluable," he says. "Also, a radio campaign in a larger market can be expensive, but with proper planning it can be a worthwhile investment."

In any multimedia campaign, Penninger emphasizes the need to set aside funds to ensure a memorable and impactful result. An ill-conceived or poorly produced campaign, regardless of the schedule you run, could waste your valuable resources.

Source: John Penninger, Director of Marketing, Open Hand, Atlanta, GA. Phone (404) 419-3318.
E-mail: jpenninger@projectopenhand.org

Help Craft CEO's Message

Although your CEO may not be a writer, he or she is expected to write letters, speeches and messages to supporters on a regular basis, especially in annual reports.

You may be the one who is responsible for bringing some life to that message. To prepare written remarks that sound fresh, appropriate and anything but canned:

✓ **Know your CEO's speaking style.** Is he friendly and approachable in groups or while addressing a live audience? Does she stick to business and efficiently address each point before taking questions? The message you write should follow a similar flow.

✓ **Read letters the CEO has written.** Without asking for personal correspondence, ask to see some routine business letters your CEO wrote or dictated. Look for a common thread in phrases or salutations he/she likes to use.

✓ **Formal or folksy?** If your CEO likes to tell stories or jokes that lead to the point when speaking to groups,

mimic this technique in messages you write. Warren Buffett's Berkshire Hathaway shareholder letters and annual reports are filled with entertaining comments that never fail to become headlines the day they are released.

✓ **Interview your CEO first.** Meet to discuss points to be covered in the piece, keeping the tone conversational and informal. Write down or record amusing or enlightening comments that could be integrated into the message.

✓ **Clean up quotes without changing context.** Almost everyone differs in his or her written and verbal speaking style while saying the same thing. Be sure to give your CEO at least one opportunity to review what you have written on his or her behalf to ensure that you haven't inadvertently changed the message's intent.

✓ **Read the letter aloud to yourself or a colleague.** Ask for a critique of its flow, and rework sentences or phrases that sound stiff, cliché or insincere.

 Seven Ways to Celebrate Your Facility Dedication

A new building or addition is reason to celebrate, and the dedication of the structure provides opportunities to invite the public to see your mission in action.

The best time to begin planning your building's dedication is well before construction is complete. There are even pre-dedication events that can enhance community interest.

Here are seven ideas to create a personal, meaningful dedication event:

1. **Hold a topping-off ceremony.** Keep abreast of construction progress, and determine a time when the final structural beam will be placed. Before the crane raises the beam, have board members, key staff and supporters on hand to autograph and date the beam with permanent paint pens. Invite as many persons as construction notice permits to build interest in the approaching dedication.

2. **Plan an open house of both the new and existing facilities.** Have all departments participate by having their areas ready for visitors. Have displays, refreshments and tour guides throughout the buildings to ensure all areas are seen and traffic flow is smooth.

3. **Provide live music.** Small ensembles of singers, children's orchestras or soloists performing in various locations will draw visitors from area to area.

4. **Use photo and brochure displays near exits.** Include attractive photos of organization activities or a historical retrospective using vintage photos, as well as brochures on new programs.

5. **Show videos or films in meeting rooms or auditoriums.** If you have new or existing films of your organization in action, show as many as possible in rooms.

6. **Ask visitors to sign a scrapbook or guest book.** Have guest books for supporters to write good wishes for your organization's continued success. You will be able to use the remarks in future literature.

7. **Create a commemorative coin.** Design a metal coin with the dedication date and building silhouette. One side may have an inspirational message or your motto. Give the coin in small velour bags to all who attend.

80 Use Community Contacts When Designing Your PSA

Many large organizations use celebrities for their PSAs. While this isn't a realistic option for most nonprofits, you can make your PSA eye-catching by using local celebrities. Whether it's a well-known fire chief or your local mayor, reach out to high profile contacts for your next PSA.

Contact local reporters with whom you have a good working relationship to see if they would be interested in participating. It's possible the person you're contacting might already have a vested interest in the issue you're trying to promote and would be willing to assist you.

Get the community involved by contacting your local emergency services, schools and houses of worship to find a unique location to film your PSA that will serve to intensify your message.

81 How to Attract a Press Conference Crowd

Putting together a press conference can be daunting. Even more nerve-wracking is wondering whether anyone will show up for the big event.

The trick to rounding up reporters is to think like one, says Keith Lawrence, director of media relations, Office of News & Communications, Duke University (Durham, NC).

For starters, that means being very selective about whom you invite to your press conference, says Lawrence. A good reporter knows who can always be relied on for a quick quote, as opposed to plum sources who should only be tapped for a major story.

Likewise, you should know which members of the local media like to come out to pressers more than others, and for what topics. General-assignment reporters might be more likely to grab onto any lead, while a beat reporter will only want to be invited when missing it might mean getting scooped by another news outlet. Reporters who are tied to their desks all day long may just appreciate the chance to get out of the office. (How can you find out which kinds you're dealing with? Good, old-fashioned gumshoeing: call and ask!)

In other words, don't just hit send all on your e-mail every time you're sending out an alert, says Lawrence. "[Journalists] are only going to cover you so many times, so make sure you pick your spots carefully."

Seasoned reporters cultivate and groom sources over many years in order to gain their trust and ultimately get the most important information out of them (think of Deep Throat's involvement in the Watergate scandal). Press-conference management is also relationship-building, he says.

"Journalists will remember if you have called them to something that turns out to be a snoozer," says Lawrence. "On the flip side, if journalists trust you because you haven't led them astray in the past, they're more likely to attend when you do call a press conference."

Once a reporter shows up, your job is to provide all the information he/she needs to put together the story, says Lawrence, "Make sure all the right people are there to answer any questions that may come up." When prepping your presser, do as many journalists do and think around the story from all angles. What questions come to mind, and who are the best people from your organization to answer them?

However, also remember that different media outlets have different needs — especially TV news, says Lawrence. "If you are inviting TV, make sure there is something visual for them to film," Lawrence says, "and hold the press conference in the late morning or early afternoon, which are times typically convenient for TV news."

> ### News Release Opportunities
>
> What might justify preparing a news release for your organization? Develop a list of justifiable reasons for distributing news releases that includes these and other examples:
>
> - Appointing new employees.
> - Launching a new program or service.
> - Collaborating with another nonprofit on a program or event.
> - Achieving a milestone: most people served, an anniversary and more.
> - Bestowing honors or awards on deserving people or organizations.
> - Kicking off or ending a fundraising campaign.
> - Opening a satellite office or branch.
> - Forming partnerships with businesses and other organizations.
> - Adding new volunteers.
> - Announcing or hosting an event.
> - Changing your name or services.
> - Honoring long-time employees.
> - Citing an achievement of someone served by your organization (student, youth).
> - Announcing new board members.
> - Completing research.
> - Publicizing a major gift or grant.
> - Citing an employee's achievement.

Source: Keith Lawrence, Director of Media Relations, Duke Office of News & Communications, Durham, NC. Phone (919) 681-8059. E-mail: keith.lawrence@duke.edu. Website: www.dukenews.duke.edu

82 Stories Give Everyone a Chance to Contribute

What to do with people who are devoted to your cause but may not be in a position to write you a big check?

Let them share their stories, says Ron Cohen, vice president for university relations, Susquehanna University (Selinsgrove, PA).

The university began hosting alumni profiles under the heading, Alumni Spotlight, on the website's home page, in 2006 leading up to the university's current capital campaign. Says Cohen, "The primary message is that, in this campaign, there is an opportunity for everyone who cares about Susquehanna to make a contribution. The stories have value and are a meaningful way for people to respond, whether or not they can write a check."

The story submission process is fairly flexible, with some alumni offering to share their own stories and others being asked to do so. Alumni may write their own profiles or simply share their information and approve a draft written by university staff. Stories are only edited for grammar and to keep offensive language out. Subject matter for the profiles varies, ranging from important relationships with faculty members and/or coaches to a lifelong friendship with a roommate to a pivotal internship or research experience.

Cohen says the admissions office sees a major advantage in the profiles, scooping up several of the stronger submissions to share with prospective students and families. "In the end," he says, "it really is all about letting people know they have something valuable to give. These stories benefit the university in a number of ways."

Source: Ron Cohen, Vice President for University Relations, Susquehanna University, Selinsgrove, P.A. Phone (570) 372-4103. E-mail: cohen@susqu.edu. Website: www.susqu.edu

83 Track Your Nonprofit's News Coverage

If your media department has been diligently spreading the word about your nonprofit's annual events, one-time events or deeds of bettering the community, why not capture that coverage on your website? News coverage about your nonprofit offers power-packed information for your website and adds credibility to your cause.

Follow these tips in capturing the media coverage:

✓ **Capture video streams from local news stations to post on your organization's website.** Visual aids such as these are dynamic and allow interested parties to get the full scope of your organization's purpose.

✓ **Scan newspaper articles.** Clip and scan newspaper coverage about events, donations or your organization's philanthropy within the community.

✓ **Audio stream radio interviews that feature your**

nonprofit's leaders. Listeners can hear about your nonprofit's goals straight from the leaders themselves.

✓ **Gather press releases that your media staff has created and include them under a press release tab on your website.** This information allows researchers and news writers easy access to the latest information about what new things your organization is doing.

✓ **Create a media tab on the main page of your nonprofit's site where you can post all of the above news-related items.** This assists those interested in your organization in staying up-to-date with the latest breaking news from all mediums.

✓ **When posting media clips from radio, news or print outlets,** be sure to obtain copyright permission from the source before posting them to your site.

84 Maximize Press When Announcing New Equipment

When your organization makes a large equipment purchase with donated funds, take care to showcase not just the equipment, but its importance to furthering your mission. Doing so will reinforce donors' decisions to give to your cause and educate the community about your organization and the responsibility with which you steward gifts.

Say, for example, you are a public relations coordinator at a hospital that secures new diagnostic equipment that brings a new level of patient care to your service area. To launch a media blitz:

❑ **Educate yourself first.** When you fully understand how the equipment works, how it enhances patient care or saves lives and why it represents advancement over previous procedures, you can answer media questions with confidence and enthusiasm.

❑ **Highlight patient stories.** Equipment is impressive, but its positive impact on real people in your community draws more attention and helps better illustrate how it improves health, saves lives or shortens diagnostic time.

❑ **Spotlight staff.** Behind every cutting-edge machine is a skilled professional operator. Tell the public how you were able to obtain the equipment because physicians, nurses, radiographers or other staff have the background or qualifications to operate it.

❑ **Announce outreach accommodations.** Since your new equipment is one-of-a-kind in the region, physicians in other cities will refer patients and their families who may need to stay overnight. Tell about your partnerships with hotels, restaurants and other businesses to assist them.

❑ **Make medical staff available to media.** You may be spokesperson much of the time, but a few words from your chief of staff or department chair will carry more weight with reporters. Remind experts to avoid technical terminology when on the record.

❑ **Host a public open house.** Invite the community to view the new suite before it is being heavily used. Have a walk-through of patient and recovery areas, with staff on hand to greet and answer questions.

85 Committee Provides Heads-up to University

Big hair has been out since the early 1980s, but one thing that has kept its value since that time is the Campus Community Relations Committee (CCRC) of the University of Arizona (Tucson, AZ).

The CCRC was formed in the 1980s to foster better relationships and communication between the surrounding neighborhoods and the university campus, says Associate Vice President Jaime Gutierrez. The CCRC, Gutierrez says, "allows members to discuss issues, resolve conflicts, find and implement mutually satisfactory solutions to problems and work for the betterment of the community in an atmosphere of respect."

Here's how the committee works:

✓ Bylaws govern the proceedings and establish parameters for membership.

✓ Anyone wishing to join can petition the committee, which would then vote on whether to add another member.

✓ Regardless of membership, anyone from the community can attend the meetings and participate during a call to the audience.

✓ Members are expected to attend monthly meetings (except in June and July when CCRC does not meet). Anyone who misses three consecutive meetings is declared inactive and no longer counted for quorum purposes.

The committee can pose challenges, Gutierrez says, since members don't always agree with the university's policies. "When they disagree they are very vocal about it, but that can be a real opportunity. Having a committee in place that informs the university about potential issues of interest and conflict with the surrounding community is a valuable resource and gives the institution an opportunity to find ways to respond in a positive way."

In addition, Gutierrez says the committee understands the issues of the university on a deeper level than casual observers and at times can advocate on behalf of mutually beneficial interests.

Source: Jaime P. Gutierrez, Associate Vice President, University of Arizona, Tucson, AZ. Phone (520) 621-3316. E-mail: jaimeg@email.arizona.edu

86 Publicize Your Employees' Community Involvement

How often and in what ways are you making the public aware of your employees' involvement in the life of your community?

Part of making your case for economic impact should include making the public aware of the many ways in which your employees are playing an active role in the life of your community. Here are some examples of how you can do that:

❏ Place an ad in your local newspaper that lists your employees by name and lists how each employee is making a difference: volunteer activities, positions held on local boards and so forth.

❏ Kick off a publicity campaign with a theme: "We take pride in making [name of community] all that it can be." Include a series of feature stories that speak to your theme.

❏ Host a handful of after-work receptions in the lobbies of larger corporate offices. Ask several of your employees to attend and mingle with each corporation's employees. Get the corporate CEO to make brief remarks about your organization's level of community involvement.

❏ Include space on your website that speaks to different aspects of your employees' involvement in the community.

❏ Take the lead in hosting a community betterment summit at your facility that includes some of your employees along with community leaders and chamber of commerce representatives. Identify a handful of ways in which, together, you can work to improve the quality of life in your community.

87 Facilitate Communication With a Mobile Application

Business professionals are increasingly treating mobile phones as a primary source of information — and expecting others to do the same. This is one reason staff at the Newspaper Association of America (Arlington, VA) produced a mobile phone application specifically for their annual mediaXchange conference.

"The application provided convenient and up-to-date access to most information contained in the onsite program guide," says Kevin McCourt, vice president of advertising and exhibition sales. "The conference program, speaker and session outlines, roster of exhibitors, hotel information, and a live Twitter and blog feed with ongoing posts were all delivered to pretty much any mobile device available."

Though much of the information was available on a dedicated website, navigating it was far easier in a native mobile application than a phone-based Web browser, says McCourt.

Because the application was new to the 2010 conference, organizers made it easy to acquire, having members text a short code to a five-digit number to receive a website and instructions on how to download and install the application, or download it directly from the conference website.

Reaction to the application was uniformly enthusiastic, says McCourt. Usage statistics showed almost 50 percent of event participants using the application, with an average of more than 40 interactions per user and a 25 percent click-through rate to more information on sessions, speakers or exhibitors.

A conference survey identified the application as the second-most frequently used tool (after the conference website) in planning for and participating in the event.

While the application was developed as an in-kind service from corporate sponsors, McCourt estimates its market value at $20,000. Mobile software developer Handmark, Inc. (Kansas City, MO) conceived and delivered the application in about 90 days.

When developing a mobile application, McCourt advises starting early to ensure time for testing and tweaking it prior to your launch date.

Source: Kevin McCourt, Vice President of Advertising and Exhibition Sales, Newspaper Association of America. Arlington, VA. Phone (571) 366-1055. E-mail: mccourt@naa.org

88 Twitter Generates a Buzz Over Event

Toronto's techie community banded together to organize HoHoTO (Toronto, Ontario, Canada) using Twitter (www. twitter.com) as the driving force to generate buzz about the December 2008 event, which drew the attention of the technology, marketing and public relations professional communities and raised $25,000 for the local food bank.

Michael O'Connor Clarke, vice president of Thornley Fallis Communications (Toronto, Ontario, Canada), talks about HoHoTO and how it became a success with less than two weeks of planning:

How many people attended the event?

"There have actually been two HoHoTO events. The first in December 2008, and a recent summer party we threw together on a whim in August. Pronounced 'hoe hoe TEE oh' — TO stands for the affectionate local nickname for Toronto, 'the big T.O.' — the first event drew close to 650 people raising $25,000 with just a little more than 15 days of planning. The August event drew 500 and raised $13,000."

To whom and how many was information transmitted via Twitter?

"It's really hard to say how many people we reached through Twitter. We sent out simple messages to let friends and followers know we were working on this insane plan to host a huge charity party, with about 15 days of prep time. Our friends helped spread the word. Friends of friends spread it further.

"This is the network effect of Twitter at its best. From initial messages posted to Twitter by a handful of us, it went viral. At a couple of points in the run up to the first event, and on the night of the event itself, the name of the event was the top trending topic on Twitter. Trending topics are Twitter's way of tracking big news items and other daily themes that emerge when a large group of people online are all talking about the same thing. People logging into the main Twitter home page or using one of a number of the popular third-party Twitter tools would have seen the HoHoTO topic rising to the top. Many Twitter users then asked on Twitter what HoHoTO was, further spreading the word."

Why was the Twitter marketing campaign so successful?

"First, the group of people behind HoHoTO are well-connected people in the Toronto (and broader) online community, yet each of us also has a particular area of influence. One of the key HoHoTO team members and our de facto leader, for example, is Rob Hyndman, a technology lawyer. I've been in the tech business my entire life, and know many of the people Rob knows in Toronto and elsewhere, but we also have big networks that don't overlap.

"Our organizing team included a diverse group of people — including the nonprofit sector, professional photography community, music business professionals and many more — with big personal networks and local influence among certain related but very different communities. The only thing we had in common is that we are all enthusiastic social media users, big Twitter fans and self-confessed geeks. This set of connections helped us spread the word far and fast.

"Secondly, the idea. I think we just struck a chord. Toronto was in the thick of the downturn and in that grey, miserable, not-quite-winter time of the year. People wanted an excuse to party and celebrate the vibrant geek community in Toronto.

"Third, the cause. There had been quite a bit of news about the plight of the local food banks in the run up to the holidays. This galvanized us and made it easy to get powerful messages of need across to the community."

How much potentially was saved by marketing via Twitter versus standard marketing methods?

"Thousands. We did no real marketing at all. We used e-mail between team members, a Google Groups setup (like an instant intranet) and Twitter as our communications tools, marketing channels and project management essentials. There were some costs involved in staging the event, but we managed to convince almost everyone to give us their services or products for free as in-kind donations."

Source: Michael O'Connor Clarke, Vice President, Thornley Fallis Communications, HoHoTO, Toronto, Ontario, Canada. Phone (416) 471-8664. E-mail: mocc@thornleyfallis.com

89   Make Groundbreaking Magic

Launching a major building project? To maximize participation in your groundbreaking by the media and community:

- **Start with the architect's rendering.** Use the drawing in press releases and a fundraising brochure with an envelope for pledges. Include facts of how the building will enhance services.

- **Ask supporters and employees to fill a time capsule.** A groundbreaking can be more fun with the burial of a time capsule full of items significant to your history. Invite attendees to also sign a banner to put inside to involve them in this memorable event.

- **Invite a local or regional celebrity.** Ideally, this person will have some interest in your mission and be able to make brief remarks. Present him/her with a decorated shovel or hard hat and take plenty of photos for later use.

- **Pour a cement slab.** Then let attendees leave a thumb-print, their initials, a colorful stone or other memento. The slab can be set someplace inside or outside the new structure. Have soap, water, towels and lotion on hand for post-impression cleanup.

- **Hold an outdoor picnic.** Have a large tent, refreshments, games, speeches and even a contest for a facility name if one hasn't been chosen. Offer toy shovels for children and let them break ground themselves — a great photo opportunity!

- **Take an aerial photo of this major, memorable event.** Ask everyone attending to form a circle, holding hands if there are enough people, around the perimeter of the building's future walls. Instead of construction crews' stakes or flags, use colorful ribbons and posts. Your dignitaries can stand in the center to turn over the first shovels of dirt. Write a speech that promotes future, hope and unity to be read by your speaker.

 90   Five Ways to Maximize Major Event Publicity

Some special events impact your organization beyond a mere press release, and you hope to maximize the positive attention they bring. Develop a variety of ways to share the news with different audiences, but in different ways.

1. **Client testimonials.** Your organization has been named top provider of services in your field by an independent group. Ask some of the most compelling clients you have served to go on camera or on the record for commercials, advertisements and feature stories that you can use at intervals throughout the year.

2. **Spotlight your benefactors.** A longtime supporter has left your institution a bequest that will allow you to build an addition, or ensures continuity of services for years to come. Who is or was this person? Write an article about his or her life, association with your organization and reasons for choosing you for this major gift. Explain how it will positively impact the community.

3. **First in the region.** Being first to obtain life-saving equipment, whether at the fire station or in the operating room, is a claim to fame you can enjoy even after competitors have caught up. Develop a brief but descriptive tag line to use on all publications and advertising for as long as applicable, or until you have a new first to promote.

4. **Host a celebration activity.** Invite the community to share in your good fortune by holding an open house, family festival or free concert that trumpets your good news while also showing your gratitude. Publicity for the event should center on the reason for the celebration, and result in free media coverage.

5. **Award a scholarship.** Helping a deserving student who has a connection to your organization is an excellent way to express thanks for community support that led to your achievement. Media coverage about the recipient also will bounce back to the reason you founded the scholarship in the first place.

Lightning Source UK Ltd.
Milton Keynes UK
UKOW06f2121020913

216389UK00008B/181/P